The Sexual Scene

*Trans-*action Books

TA-1 Campus Power Struggle/ *Howard S. Becker*

TA-2 Cuban Communism/ *Irving Louis Horowitz*

TA-3 The Changing South/ *Raymond W. Mack*

TA-4 Where Medicine Fails/ *Anselm L. Strauss*

TA-5 The Sexual Scene/ *John H. Gagnon, William Simon*

TA-6 Black Experience:
Soul/ *Lee Rainwater*

TA-7 Black Experience:
The Transformation of Activism/ *August Meier*

TA-8 Law and Order:
Modern Criminals/ *James F. Short, Jr.*

TA-9 Law and Order:
The Scales of Justice/ *Abraham S. Blumberg*

TA-10 Social Science and National Policy/ *Fred R. Harris*

TA-11 Peace and the War Industry/ *Kenneth E. Boulding*

TA-12 America and the Asian Revolutions/ *Robert Jay Lifton*

The Sexual Scene

Edited by
JOHN H. GAGNON/WILLIAM SIMON

Trans-**action** Books

Published and distributed by
Aldine Publishing Company

The essays in this book originally appeared
in *Trans-action* Magazine

TA Book-5
Library of Congress Catalog Number: 72-96128

Contents

Preface   vii

Introduction:
Perspectives on the Sexual Scene   1
John H. Gagnon/William Simon

Psychosexual Development   23
William Simon/John H. Gagnon

How and Why America's Sex Standards Are Changing   43
Ira L. Reiss

Hippie Morality—More Old Than New   59
Bennett M. Berger

The Horseless Cowboys   75
John A. Popplestone

Our Unlovable Sex Laws   81
Fred Rodell

Abortion Laws and Their Victims   91
Alice S. Rossi

Sexual Assaults in the Philadelphia Prison System   107
Alan J. Davis

Lesbian Liaisons   125
David A. Ward/Gene G. Kassebaum

Pornography—Raging Menace or Paper Tiger?   137
John H. Gagnon/William Simon

Preface

However diverse their attitudes and interpretations may
sometimes be, social scientists are now entering a period
of shared realization that the United States—both at home
and abroad—has entered a crucial period of transition.
Indeed, the much burdened word "crisis" has now become
a commonplace among black militants, Wall Street lawyers,
housewives, and even professional politicians.

For the past six years, *Trans*-action magazine has dedicated itself to the task of reporting the strains and conflicts
within the American system. But the magazine has done
more than this. It has pioneered in social programs for
changing the society, offered the kind of analysis that has
permanently restructured the terms of the "dialogue" between peoples and publics, and offered the sort of prog-
nosis that makes for real alterations in social and political
policies directly affecting our lives.

The work done in the pages of *Trans*-action has crossed

disciplinary boundaries. This represents much more than simple cross-disciplinary "team efforts." It embodies rather a recognition that the social world cannot be easily carved into neat academic disciplines. That, indeed, the study of the experience of blacks in American ghettos, or the manifold uses and abuses of agencies of law enforcement, or the sorts of overseas policies that lead to the celebration of some dictatorships and the condemnation of others, can best be examined from many viewpoints and from the vantage points of many disciplines.

This series of books clearly demonstrates the superiority of starting with real world problems and searching out practical solutions, over the zealous guardianship of professional boundaries. Indeed, it is precisely this approach that has elicited enthusiastic support from leading American social scientists for this new and dynamic series of books.

The demands upon scholarship and scientific judgment are particularly stringent, for no one has been untouched by the current situation. Each essay republished in these volumes bears the imprint of the author's attempt to communicate his own experience of the crisis. Yet, despite the sense of urgency these papers exhibit, the editors feel that many have withstood the test of time, and match in durable interest the best of available social science literature. This collection of *Trans*-action articles, then, attempts to address itself to immediate issues without violating the basic insights derived from the classical literature in the various fields of social science.

The subject matter of these books concerns social changes that have aroused the long-standing needs and present-day anxieties of us all. These changes are in organizational life styles, concepts of human ability and intelligence, changing patterns of norms and morals, the relationship of social conditions to physical and biological environments, and in the status of social science with national policy making.

This has been a decade of dissident minorities, massive shifts in norms of social conduct, population explosions and urban expansions, and vast realignments between nations of the world. The social scientists involved as editors and authors of this *Trans*-action series have gone beyond observation of these critical areas, and have entered into the vital and difficult tasks of explanation and interpretation. They have defined issues in a way making solutions possible. They have provided answers as well as asked the right questions. Thus, this series should be conceived as the first collection dedicated not to the highlighting of social problems alone, but to establishing guidelines for social solutions based on the social sciences.

THE EDITORS
Trans-action

Perspectives on the Sexual Scene

JOHN H. GAGNON/WILLIAM SIMON

In the last half century sex has moved from the dim background of American life to occupy nearly the entire center stage. Few other topics occupy either directly or indirectly so much of the leisure time of the waking life (and perhaps the dreaming life) of vast segments of the society. Entire industries spend much of their time trying to organize presentations around sexual themes or try to hook products onto a potential sexual moment or success. That there has been a radical shift in the quantity and quality of sexual presentations in the society cannot be denied. However, the evidence about what effect this shift will have on the society and what directions we will move toward in the future is only fragmentary.

In certain periods of American history, when Freud was revolutionary and Kinsey only beginning his work, no one had any idea what anyone else was doing or feeling and because of this pluralistic ignorance it was possible to believe

in a natural order in sexual matters. After all sex was ultimately biological and hence natural; it was something that
flowered and grew, if not mutilated by the society or cultural repression. It is this vision of the naturalness of sex
that still dominates much of our concern with the sexual
world. The largest bodies of knowledge that have been
generated about the sexual—and how little there still is—
still derive from the "natural." One need only point out
the biological commitments of Freud, the zoological concerns of Kinsey and the medical framework of Masters
and Johnson.

The public discussion of the sexual in the West is only
some 70 years old in its vaguer outlines, and for American
society, perhaps, only as old as the publication of Kinsey's
first volume in 1948. This lack of an historical dimension
(a lack that exists in nearly every domain of life except
for the folklore that passes for history textbooks) is most
pervasive in the sexual area. In an important sense this
too is a consequence of the belief in the naturalness of sex.
The material only has to be recorded once and never has to
be taught, hence everyone is required to reinvent the past
or at least reassemble unselfconsciously the old material
into what they think are new forms. It is this point that is
central to Bennet Berger's discussion of hippie morality.
The hippie movement in its rather diffuse ideology has put
together a series of postures on sexual and social matters
that are nearly identical with the antibourgeosie positions
of the bohemians of the 1920s. At the same time the
historical conditions under which the two movements have
developed have been quite different. The bohemianism of
the 1920s remained marginal to the larger culture, becoming a transitory social location for the alienated. As an
encapsulated social location, existing only by reputation to
the bourgeosie that they hoped to provoke, bohemia in

Greenwich Village was a protected environment allowing the development of talent and the gradual reentry into the society of its members. The hippie movement, on the other hand, became the center of mass public interest and the margins of the movement were constantly penetrated by the social scientist, the social journalist and the weekend hippie. Before the movement took on a well-defined or original posture it became a form of entertainment for the larger society. The immediacy of the mass media forced the rest of the society to react to hippieness nearly instantly. This process means that subcultures no longer have significant periods of social isolation during which ideologies may be developed. At the same time the bohemian-hippie ideology has greater power to spread itself because it is magnified through the media to all parts of the country and to all those who are even provisionally alienated.

The increasing significance of the sexual in modern life has been greeted with joy by a few, despair by a few and an ambivalence by the many. Those who are joyous believe that we are now confronting a rare opportunity for individual growth and personal maturity through the unleashing of the sexual potential. The despairing find the increased significance of sex a portent of a disintegrating social order. The vast majority in the society who do not have much of an ideological commitment one way or another on the sexual question are made uneasy by what they think is going on. There is a general agreement, however, that there is profound change occurring and that this change will be of major consequence to the society.

This experience of change, especially with respect to the mass media and the freedom of discussion of sexual activity, has led to a belief in the existence of a sex revolution. What may be revolutionary or may set the stage for revolution, however, is the eager willingness of the society to embrace the idea that a revolution is going on. Yet to discuss changes in sexual behavior as if these behaviors were self-contained, that is, influencing only other sexual activities or influenced only by previous sexual training, is to become lost in the world of pornotopia. That is a world in which the sexual exists stripped of social meaning and psychological investment, without either a past or a future, merely a set of glands and organs with universal significance and universal consequences. Discussion of the sexual should begin to move us out of this never-neverland where the only psychological categories are guilt and shame or joy and ecstasy, and the only moral categories are those of orthodox conscience.

There is, however, a dual aspect of sexuality that generates complexity in both sexual activity and social regulation of it. The sexual dimension links man to his evolution and gives him a sense of participation in species life and species survival. The sexual component also remains a powerful reminder of the mediating and limit-setting functions of the body. But perhaps most important, man's sexuality can be an equally powerful reminder of how unnatural and unprogrammed the human experience is. We need only look across cultures or through the histories of single cultures to see the impressive variety of adaptations and meanings that are possible. For in acting upon his sexuality, man simultaneously celebrates one of his most universal aspects and his utter dependence upon the sociocultural moment. What, after all, is more unnatural to most of our contemporaries than the nude human body in a sexual posture?

There have been radical changes in the definition or representation of sex in American cultural life since the second World War, but these changes have picked up enormous momentum in the period 1964 to 1970. These changes at the public level of the society are easily discerned and listed, but what is more complex is the way in which such changes in the public domain can come to influence behavior in the private realm. Such translation from public to private does not require a concordance between publically expressed attitudes and private behavior or a necessary relationship between what is going on in the movies and what people do in bed, but rather more subtly the relationship between mass media and the mechanisms by which symbolic presentations come to create shifts in beliefs, attitudes and behavior at the private level.

As we have noted before, as a result of a nationwide media system, the society has a more erotic tone than it has ever had before. This erotization of the environment has two dimensions, one more exotic than the other and perhaps the less important. The first dimension involves the degree to which the public domain is invaded by representations of the sexual that were not only not permissible in public previously, but were conceived to be deviant, immoral or criminal behaviors even when married individuals indulged in them in private. (See Rodell for the current legal situation.) In the play *Futz!* the hero loves (both emotionally and physically) a sow. In the plays *Che* and *The Beard* and in the film *I am Curious (Blue)* acts of mouth genital contact are graphically depicted. The magazine *Playboy* has for the first time published pictures of female pubic hair (a barrier that had been breached by other publications, but none so prestigious). Some part of this growing permissiveness is a direct result of the activities of the federal judiciary in handling a number of major cases involving erotic materials (see Gagnon and Simon). The courts seem at one level to be somewhat ahead of the social consensus (and perhaps even the office of the President) in this more permissive attitude, but there are substantial continuities involved between the production and consumption of culture in this society. Both the popular and the more traditional arts have been living in closer accord with and collaboration with what had been their underground. The degree of continuity between what was erotic or pornographic in the visual arts and the high arts displayed in museums is far greater than ever before. The sexualization of Pop Art through the erotic use of the comic-book figure is apparent as is the use of new plastic materials that have a greater degree of sensuality. The "nudie" or "skin flic" film have elements that now appear with regularity in major Hollywood productions.

One indicator of how far we have come is the fact that *The New York Times* in 1948 refused to carry the conservative Philadelphia medical publishing-house advertisement for the first Kinsey volume. By the middle 1960s *The Times* was carrying, without blushing, advertisements for books which had previously been unavailable outside the locked library cabinets of Kinsey's Institute for Sex Research.

While the boundaries of the publically available have changed enormously, this only indirectly suggests what the society will utilize, the degree to which it will be utilized or the final form that available materials will take. Contrary to the censors' predictions, the increasing permissiveness of the media have not resulted in major behavioral changes or a flood of people moving to the erotic margins (see Ira Reiss for the state of the premarital barricade of the sexual revolution).

It is this second dimension of the erotization of the society that is the most important: it is the extent to which the sexual enters into conventional public discourse, without necessarily creating new images or language. The new is as often created by the process of connecting older images as by the inventing of new images. In this area we can see a profound increase in the concern for the sexual. Consumer advertising, the popular arts, the midcult sources of information such as women's magazines and TV documentaries—all provide occasion and language for thinking about and discussing sex in social situations. The two Kinsey reports are primary examples of this form of the legitimization of sexual discussion. These two volumes, published in 1948 and 1953, had limited scientific consequence when they were published, but they moved the sexual into the zone of permissible discussion. To that generation of American intellectuals who felt they had been liberated sexually through psychoanalysis, they seemed to be intolerably boring and slightly inhuman in their statistical massiveness, but for the rest of American society they became a necessary occasion for the discussion of sex. Penis, vagina, and orgasm became words that could be used, at least possibly, in conventional social situations. The Kinsey volumes are evidence for the nonlinear and open-ended quality of social change. Conceived and presented as science, they became major components of popular culture during the decade 1948 to 1958. At the same time the presentation of sex in this essentially statistical landscape sufficiently decreased the affect normally attendant upon discussion of sex, so that nonerotic conversations could take place about sex. It was exactly the qualities that intellectuals disliked about the Kinsey volumes that allowed them to have consequence for larger segments of the population.

Playboy Magazine also illustrates the significance of sex becoming part of normal public discourse and the unintended ways in which mass media documents are used by the public. *Playboy* is an explicitly sexual document for many people. After all, there are pictures of nearly naked girls, sometimes frolicking about with men, clips from naked sequences in movies, and cartoons and jokes playing on the sexual. Yet when the magazine was first published there were a large number of others nearly identical with *Playboy* in its sexual aspect. Yet, of all of these magazines, *Playboy* has survived to become nearly a national institution. This is essentially because the magazine has taken for itself the role of legitimating not sexual behavior, but what Ernest Burgess has called sexual conduct. It is the equivalent of the *Boy Scout Manual* for the young adult, telling both males and females the etiquette of sexual activity, creating (highly conventional to be sure) scripts for the playing out of sexual dramas. It legitimates success, palliates failure, creates a rhetoric of explanation and motive and ensconces the sexual inside a social context which, because it is affluent and successful, serves to create legitimacy for the sexual activities themselves. *Playboy's* impact is not in the realm of providing masturbatory fantasy, though it probably does do that, but of providing a social context inside of which sexual desires may be thought of and in some measure acted out.

As a result of these two dimensions of the eroticization of the social environment (the public presentation of the erotic and the mechanisms of the integration of the sexual into conventional life-styles) we live in what is increasingly an erotic landscape. As a consequence, it is increasingly difficult to separate that which is expressive of disturbed fantasies and aroused anxieties from that which is descriptive of the present and/or prototypical of the future. One senses a shift from the questions about the legitimacy of what one is doing to a concern for what more it is possible to do. While present behavior still carries its burden of guilt and anxiety and requires the invocation of stabilizing norms, at the same time nagging at the edge of consciousness is the question of what more one should want to do.

The introduction of sexual images into the society both in their public and private forms has created a contradictory and confusing situation. Different segments of the society come to the sexual with profoundly different needs and even the intended content of the media is relatively unstable in its intentions. Adults come to this newly sexual landscape with an impoverished sexual imagery, and the older the adult, the more powerful a single glimpse of the erotic is thought to be. It is these people who are most invested with the theory of the power of the sexual drive and the perniciousness of pornography. They also tend to believe the more exotic descriptions of the sexual presented in the media. The young on the other hand, with their ahistorical arrogance, are more likely to find the current sexual landscape unexceptional and notice the repressive past only through the anxieties and incompletions of their parents. The contrast between the asexual quality of most familial environments and the media world must be striking. As a consequence of this ahistorical quality the young are left to reinvent the past (a task that may well not be as bad as those who believe in the moral lessons of history might think) both in potentially revolutionary ways as hippies or in the private anxieties of adolescence ("Am I the only person who ever masturbated?").

At the same time as the populations who receive the messages vary, the messages themselves are contradictory. In the wake of the publication of Masters' and Johnson's powerful study of orgasm in the female, the ladies' magazines appear to have established the legitimacy, if not the necessity, of orgasm on the part of females almost before they have established the necessity or legitimacy of intercourse. But that is just the point, for we can talk more easily about the experience of orgasm without referring to the contexts (physical, psychological or social) which produce the experience of orgasm. In this movement away from the conventional content of most sexual lives (masturbation, heterosexual petting and coitus, mostly in marriage, are the dominant sexual activities of the society) we find discussions of the exotic before we understand the conventional. Wife-swapping is discussed almost as if it were a social problem. One senses that there is more talk about wife-swapping than there is wife-swapping and that the rates of participation are extremely marginal. The structure of talk about sex has an extremely complicated relationship to behavior, and even when the structure of talk changes there is little evidence of behavior following in any direct manner.

This is especially true of the young, whose premarital behavior has become the nearly obsessive concern of the older generation. Large segments of society are organized to repress their behavior, to socialize it properly or to make it responsible, while the young themselves seem in many ways to be continuing relatively conventional patterns that existed in prior generations (again see Ira Reiss). Our concern with the sexuality of the young may not arise so much out of a sexual motive, but rather a jealousy of the young on the part of the older generation and a tendency to live through the young's experience (how much of adult Pop culture is a reflection of youthful invention in combination with adult commercial enterprise?). The sexual is a zone of behavior that can be defined as containing dramatic elements of sin or salvation so that the behavior of the young can be invested with the same elements. The content of youth culture as dramatic or revolutionary is probably as much a function of mass media presentations about the young as it is the behavior of the young.

Another point to remember is that significant social change does not come about only when there have been changes in overt behavior patterns. The moment of change may simply be the point at which new forms of behavior appear plausible. An example of this phenomenon of the increased plausibility of a behavior without behavioral change is the current status of homosexuality as a public topic. There is no evidence that there has been a growth in the proportion of the population with homosexual preferences. Clearly, there has been an increase in numbers along with the general increase in the population, but outside of certain localized centers where there tends to be in-migration, little has changed in the patterns of enlistment into homosexuality or the character of the daily life of the homosexual. He still faces the risks of arrest, convictions or imprisonment and the more frequent costs of rejection by friend, family or loss of employment.

Nevertheless, in recent years homosexuality has become one of the standard fares on the frontiers of the American cultural scene. It is popular on the part of the more paranoid to attribute this to an international homosexual conspiracy or a local theatrical homosexual conspiracy. However, as homosexuality becomes a pivotal theme in an increasing number of novels, plays, and motion pictures and as it is covered in television, newspapers and magazines, this suggests that both the recognized content of homosexuality and the dramatic or moral situations that it represents can be assimilated by mass audiences. Homosexuality becomes a vehicle for the expression of impotence, nobility through sacrifice, the problems of mental health, or the loss of love. The fact of these presentations indicates that homosexuality is differentially perceived by the society and perhaps, if we could be optimistic, might be treated more rationally. And in an important sense, if homosexuality is treated more rationally, it may lead to shifts in the manner with which the society deals with and thinks about the heterosexual.

All of these representations of the sexual, both in the public and private domain—be they of the homosexual, the alleged youthful vanguard of the sexual revolution, the female doubly liberated by the pill and the language of the multiple orgasm—may represent a watershed where both the status and the content of sexuality can be transformed. Unless one is still committed to the imagery of the natural in the area of sex (and it is an image that still contains considerable power) one must shift one's attention to the more profound roots of sexuality in order to determine the way in which these new contents will be integrated into the present processes by which sexuality is formed.

The development of sexual behavior is dominated by the sociocultural (see Simon and Gagnon). The learning of sexual behavior is learned as all behavior is learned—through the complex interaction of cultural and psychological factors. This means that sexual behavior can be expressive of a wide range of nonsexual motives and interests. The process by which the sexual is learned and its linkage to nonsexual activities creates a situation in which a heightened awareness of the sexual dimension does not necessarily lead to an incorporation of the awareness into an ongoing sexual commitment.

The primary controlling element in the development of sexual commitments is the development of gender identity. Not only does gender identity produce the appropriate code for the performance of sexual acts, but its existence is probably a necessary precursor for the development of an image of the self as sexual. Gender role in this connection has two dimensions. The first is, what kinds of sexual acts are consistent with what kinds of commitments to masculinity and feminity? Second is, what kinds of sexual role characteristics make it possible for a person to see someone else as potentially erotic? As these gender roles undergo change we may expect changes in sexual patterns far more dramatic than those induced through changes in the public imagery of sex. Although they have effects on sexual activity, the public changes are more often channeled by the more powerful forces of gender identity. One of the questions about which there is a serious lack of data is the way in which the public images will effect the way in which gender identities are formed. As we noted before, one element in this may be the large discrepancy between the gender-forming training in the home and the more permissive handling of sexual matters in the public media. Such discrepancies may well be noted by quite young children who see sex on television and then are shut off by their parents in terms of an open discussion of sex. This may result in creating mistrust and a consequent decline in the capacity of parents to impress their own sexual injunctions on their children. In this way other injunctions about gender role behavior may be loosened.

Impressionistically there does seem to be a tendency for greater tolerance of gender role deviance. The traditional stereotypic and narrow role performances of the male and female seem in some areas to be loosening. The direction of the loosening, however, does not seem to be in the direction of movement toward females taking over male role performance, but rather at this state of development a decreasing rigidity in role performances on the part of males. There has been for some time (at least two generations) a shift of this sort at the higher socio-economic levels, and the size of this segment of the society has been growing as a result of affluence. In addition, this segment of the society has long had a disproportionate capacity to shape the public images of private life and valued behavior, as well as creating some aspects of the appropriate content of the individual self-image. The middle-class young are presently mixing gender symbols more freely, with a changed commitment to hair and dress styles. In addition many of the young people today seem to have a greater and earlier capacity for *heterosociality* which may have profound consequences for the quality of heterosexual commitments. At the same time as there is a softening of the rigidities of gender role commitment for some portion of the population (the middle-class young), and their emulators (young adults and middle-class parents) there is an opposite trend in the development of increasingly cosmetic masculine presentations. Certain forms of costuming and personal style suggest that the reaction of some males to changes in the occupational realm has been an increase in traditional masculine presentations. There is a similar pattern in the motorcycle clubs that characterize lower-middle-class populations. In Popplestone's language (following Wilhelm Reich) this costuming represents a form of body armor. Due to variations in the attributes of populations who are recipients of the changing sexual styles there is a wide variation in the way that they are reacting. What is apparent is that there are some trends which are decreasing the role of sex as a test of gender commitment and even the pattern of cosmetic presentation of the motorcycle-rider or cowboy contains within it the knowledge that the behavior is role performance and not necessarily permanent.

Outside of these cosmetic adaptations, which receive the most attention, there exists the traditional pattern of growing up sexually. For many, including most of the young, sex performance and gender role performance still are firmly linked. For many males the fear of sociosexual inadequacy and incompetence and for the female the double

fear of being either too much or too little sexual will produce a continuation of the present pattern of sexual development. However, the trends that we noted earlier do
represent (in both the public and private domain as well
as in gender training) a countervailing pressure or set of
opportunities and a prospect for increasing the coolness
of the sexual area.

These trends do not suggest that there will be an immediate change in the kinds of, or frequencies with which
people do sexual things. The important changes will be
in style and attitude rather than in behavior. If there is
a significant cooling off in the sexual area, what we can
expect is that the sexual may be required to stand for less
than it does right now. Thus, rather than being a test of
social efficacy, it can be a response to the more muted expressions of the body that are currently submerged by
social need. This in turn might create a situation of
greater casualness toward sex both in terms of style and
frequency. Such a change does not mean that there will
be an increase in sexuality. On the contrary, a reduction
in the overdetermined nature of sexual experience may
lessen a commitment to sexual expression among those for
whom it is currently a test, an imperative or an ordeal.

For the time being, therefore, new patterns will strain
for accommodation with older patterns. Adolescent boys
will continue to make strong commitments to their own
sexuality by masturbating and by spinning complex fantasies. For most of them, masturbation, as commitment
and rehearsal, will continue to be organized around fantasy
themes that feed directly from their own sense of emerg-
ing masculinity. This sense of masculinity will tend to be
aggressive and direct in ways that will almost never find
expression in heterosocial communication. Among middle-
class groups, however, there will also be strong pulls toward

engagement in sociosexual activity as success on this level wins social support and social reward.

This commitment to overwhelming masculinity and rigid role definition will carry over especially into those populations untouched by affluence. An aggressive commitment to heterosexuality in a homosocial context can result in the kind of homosexuality noted in the sexual assaults in the Philadelphia prisons. Here previously aggressive men deprived of sources of masculine validation represented in sexual relationships with woman, deprived also of the capacity to express masculinity by the stripping processes of prison, used sexual assaults as mechanisms for reasserting masculine feelings. In this case homosexual acts were redefined as heterosexual by seeing the person who is assaulted as weak, submissive and therefore womanish. As long as one is sexually aggressive the relationship is by nature heterosexual, since these are the rigid terms in which male-female relationships are seen by these men. Thus, the homosexual behavior must be seen as a symbolic act of resistance on the part of men deprived of interpersonal power rather than sexual deprivation. The sexual component is the vehicle for the expression of control, a primitive form of political rather than sexual engagement.

For girls, on the other hand, there is little reason to expect a shift toward increased sexual activity, whether masturbatory or sociosexual, during the early or even middle years of adolescence. They will continue to learn how to appear sexual and will receive social support and rewards for the appearance of sexuality without performance. Indeed, the involvement in sexual activity for females at these ages may well be costly rather than rewarding. The pervasive character of female socialization may be seen even in the pattern of deviance noted in Ward and Kassebaum. Women deprived of the world of normal gratifications (as were the men in the Philadelphia prisons) move into quasi-permanent dyadic relationships in which role relationships are only partially modeled on heterosociality. Here once again the sexual activity is expressive of a wider range of desires than the sexual: love, affection and stability of expectations. In a social system stripped of any other source of relating except the body, the sexual takes on the significance that it did not have for these women before imprisonment and will not after.

Many of the facets of sexuality that we have considered are related to major shifts in the life-styles and public values of the American middle class. In a situation where decisions that commit the total society—such as the tragedy of Vietnam or even factors that affect the immediate quality of community life—appear remote to most people, the sexual takes on a significance and power beyond that which is intrinsic to it. Nowadays one strives for competence and self-actualization which, as goals, are far more flexible than the traditional achievement that one sought before. In fact, the so-called new morality involves a shift from the morality of significant acts to the morality of personal competence. Sexuality gives the individual at least the sense of making moral decisions. Not only may his sense of personal effectiveness thus be enhanced but his focus is shifted from the act to the quality of his motives. This takes the form of personal competence. Management of sexuality, as a consequence, becomes significant in self-identity. The negative aspect is that sexuality increasingly must demonstrate achievement and competence. Whether a relatively limited sexual capacity can sustain such additional burdens is questionable; we still cannot put that very private capacity into the competition for social reward and validation.

The movement of the sexual out of the domain of the

publically significant and moral into the domain of the privately moral and individual begins to shift radically the relationship between sex and the law. For the most part, the law neither dissuades nor does it prevent much of sexual activity. It commonly operates as a minefield that the unlucky, the inept or the foolish fail to negotiate. As long as sexuality stood for larger moral postures, hell-fire and damnation, or as a central element in a public passion play of good and evil, the legal postures could be supported regardless of their efficacy in controlling behavior. They represented the collective will of the society. As the morality of sexuality tends to move from the public to the private arena (following the consenting behavior between adults model) then the laws themselves seem less important and less necessary.

As the same time that the law erodes in its moral capacity to evoke a conforming response, there is still a living past that constrains and punishes those who are caught by the byproducts of sexual activity. This is especially manifest in the problems faced by women who wish abortions. The law in this case constrains those who have a monopoly of medical service, but does not constrain these women, the majority of whom are married, from trying to control the number of children that they have. In double sense, in the case of abortion, the price is exacted for getting caught. Since men never pay the moral and emotional cost of abortion it is often difficult to organize them to aid in reform of the legal machinery. Further the absolute control by a female in choosing whether to give birth or not is another element shifting the balance of power between man and women in the society. What Alice Rossi's article makes us confront is that while the society entertains itself at the erotic margins with suppressing or enjoying pornography and other epiphenomena, tragic historical inequities exist in the legal structure.

The constant affluence experienced by the American middle class since World War II also creates certain pressures on sexuality. The affluent young, who have only the most abstract notions about nonaffluence and poverty, increasingly demand that the landscape on the other side of traditional achievement be described in terms that make sense as experience, for affluence generates a kind of anomie all its own. The ease and abundance with which certain goals are achieved trivialize the goals. One response to the anomie of affluence, as seen long ago by Durkheim, is a quest for new, more intense experience. Something of this phenomenon can be seen in the pursuit of drug experience by many middle-class young people. Sexuality obviously is a key way-station in the pursuit of intense experience.

In the long run, both the trends for personal competence and for intense experiences should encourage all of society —young and not-so-young—to become even more concerned with sex, more sexually active and possibly more sexually experimental. This suggests not only a narrowing of gender distinctions but quite possibly a narrowing of generational distinctions. Parents and children might increasingly share sexual style and commitment as the young become sexual earlier and the old remain sexual and younger longer. Generational difference could erode considerably, and in fact, may already have begun to do so.

Although exotic and marginal sex is at center stage, most sexual activity still is aimed at family formation and maintenance. But as the imagery of sex changes, there are changes in the character of the family and in its relation to the larger society. Students of family life have for some time commented upon the narrowing of family control and the shift of socializing functions among the young to places outside the home. Along with these changes, new weight has been given to interpersonal attachments—as against external constraints—in the maintenance of a viable family life. Again, sexuality is taking new relevance; it may have to serve as both content and visible proof of enduring attachment. This is seen in the emphasis now placed upon sexual competence in marriage, one that borders on sexual athleticism.

This poses a difficulty. One still finds it hard to get social recognition and support for his sexual competence in marriage. For many, making competent conversation about sex becomes a bid for this social recognition. This is reflected in the growing demand for technical and pseudo-technical information. The results are mixed. Some find reassurance in their verbal performance. Yet, the more one talks sex, the more detail one has against which to compare his direct sexual experience. This does not always enhance one's sense of competence or even one's identity.

In general, the sexual dimension in our society comprises a limited biological capacity that is harnessed and amplified by varied social uses. Within that context we have sketched both possible uses and modes of amplification. We have emphasized that the expression of the sexual component is the celebration of a social and psychological drama rather than a natural response. We have suggested that there may be substantial change in this social drama. In the past the drama has been a silent charade. Now we appear to be giving the drama a sound track and inviting the audience to participate. Competence increasingly replaces guilt as the major source for amplifying complexity. Guilt had the power of endowing limited behavior with enduring emotions. Competence may require an enlargement of the scope of the behavior. Keynes may have to replace

Adam Smith as the metaphorical cartographer for our sexual style. Whether the principle of "the more you spend the more you have" can apply to the body any more effectively than it applies to the economy is questionable. For while physiology may not be our destinies, it can still be a major source of their frustration.

State University   *John H. Gagnon / William Simon*
Stony Brook, New York
Institute for Juvenile Research
Chicago, Illinois

Psychosexual Development

WILLIAM SIMON / JOHN H. GAGNON

Erik Erikson has observed that, prior to Sigmund Freud, "sexologists" tended to believe that sexual capacities appeared suddenly with the onset of adolescence. Sexuality followed those external evidences of physiological change that occurred concurrent with or just after puberty. Psychoanalysis changed all that. In Freud's view, libido—the generation of psychosexual energies—should be viewed as a fundamental element of human experience at least beginning with birth, and possibly before that. Libido, therefore, is essential, a biological constant to be coped with at all levels of individual, social, and cultural development. The truth of this received wisdom, that is, that sexual development is a continuous contest between biological drive and cultural restraint should be seriously questioned. Obviously sexuality has roots in biological processes, but so do many other capacities including many that involve physical and mental competence and vigor. There is, however, abundant evidence that the final states which these capacities attain escape the rigid impress of biology. This independence of biological constraint is rarely claimed for the area of sexuality, but we would like to argue that the sexual is precisely that realm where the sociocultural forms most completely dominate biological influences.

It is difficult to get data that might shed much light on the earliest aspects of these questions: Adults are hardly equipped with total recall and the pre-verbal or primitively verbal child does not have ability to report accurately on his own internal state. But it seems obvious—and it is a basic assumption of this paper—that with the beginnings of adolescence many new factors come into play, and to emphasize a straight-line developmental continuity with infant and childhood experiences may be seriously misleading. In particular, it is dangerous to assume that because some childhood behavior appears sexual to adults, it must be sexual. An infant or a child engaged in genital play (even if orgasm is observed) can in no sense be seen as experiencing the complex set of feelings that accompanies adult or even adolescent masturbation.

Therefore, the authors reject the unproven assumption that "powerful" psychosexual drives are fixed biological attributes. More importantly, we reject the even more dubious assumption that sexual capacities or experiences tend to translate immediately into a kind of universal "knowing" or innate wisdom—that sexuality has a magical ability, possessed by no other capacity, that allows biological drives to be expressed directly in psychosocial and social behaviors.

The prevailing image of sexuality—particularly that of the Freudian tradition—is that of an intense, high-pressure drive that forces a person to seek physical sexual gratification, a drive that expresses itself indirectly if it cannot be expressed directly. The available data suggest to us a different picture—one that shows either lower levels of intensity, or, at least, greater variability. We find that there are many social situations or life-roles in which reduced sex activity or even deliberate celibacy is undertaken with little evidence that the libido has shifted in compensation to some other sphere.

A part of the legacy of Freud is that we have all become remarkably adept at discovering "sexual" elements in non-sexual behavior and symbolism. What we suggest instead (following Kenneth Burke's three-decade-old insight) is the reverse—that sexual behavior can often express and serve nonsexual motives.

We see sexual behavior therefore as *scripted* behavior, not the masked expression of a primordial drive. The individual can learn sexual behavior as he or she learns other behavior—through scripts that in this case give the self, other persons, and situations erotic abilities or content. Desire, privacy, opportunity, and propinquity with an attractive member of the opposite sex are not, in themselves, enough; in ordinary circumstances, nothing sexual will occur unless one or both actors organize these elements into an appropriate script. The very concern with foreplay in sex suggests this. From one point of view, foreplay may be defined as merely progressive physical excitement generated by touching naturally erogenous zones. The authors have referred to this conception elsewhere as the "rubbing of two sticks together to make a fire" model. It would seem to be more valuable to see this activity as symbolically invested behavior through which the body is eroticized and through which mute, inarticulate motions and gestures are translated into a sociosexual drama.

A belief in the sociocultural dominance of sexual behavior finds support in cross-cultural research as well as in data restricted to the United States. Psychosexual development is universal—but it takes many forms and tempos. People in different cultures construct their scripts differently; and in our own society, different segments of the population act out different psychosexual dramas—something much less likely to occur if they were all reacting more or less blindly to the same superordinate urge. The most marked differences occur, of course, between male and female patterns of sexual behavior. Obviously, some of this is due to biological differences, including differences in hormonal functions at different ages. But the significance of social scripts predominate; the recent work of Masters and Johnson, for example, clearly points to far greater orgasmic capacities on the part of females than our culture would lead us to suspect. And within each sex—especially among men—different social and economic groups have different patterns.

Let us examine some of these variations, and see if we can decipher the scripts.

Whether one agrees with Freud or not, it is obvious that we do not become sexual all at once. There is continuity with the past. Even infant experiences can strongly influence later sexual development.

But continuity is not causality. Childhood experiences (even those that appear sexual) will in all likelihood be influential not because they are intrinsically sexual, but because they can affect a number of developmental trends, *including* the sexual. What situations in infancy—or even early childhood—can be called psychosexual in any sense other than that of creating potentials?

The key term, therefore, must remain potentiation. In infancy, we can locate some of the experiences (or sensations) that will bring about a sense of the body and its capacities for pleasure and discomfort and those that will influence the child's ability to relate to others. It is possible, of course, that through these primitive experiences, ranges are being established—but they are very broad and overlapping. Moreover, if these are profound experiences to the child—and they may well be that—they are not expressions of biological necessity, but of the earliest forms of social learning.

In childhood, after infancy there is what appears to be some real sex play. About half of all adults report that they did engage in some form of sex play as children;

and the total who actually did may be half again as many. But, however the adult interprets it later, what did it mean to the child at the time? One suspects that, as in much of childhood role-playing, their sense of the adult meanings attributed to the behavior is fragmentary and ill-formed. Many of the adults recall that, at the time, they were concerned with being found out. But here, too, were they concerned because of the real content of sex play, or because of the mystery and the lure of the forbidden that so often enchant the child? The child may be assimilating outside information about sex for which, at the time, he has no real internal correlate or understanding.

A small number of persons do have sociosexual activity during preadolescence—most of it initiated by adults. But for the majority of these, little apparently follows from it. Without appropriate sexual scripts, the experience remains unassimilated—at least in adult terms. For some, it is clear, a severe reaction may follow from falling "victim" to the sexuality of an adult—but, again, does this reaction come from the sexual act itself or from the social response, the strong reactions of others? (There is some evidence that early sexual activity of this sort is associated with deviant adjustments in later life. But this, too, may not be the result of sexual experiences in themselves so much as the consequence of having fallen out of the social main stream and, therefore, of running greater risks of isolation and alienation.)

In short, relatively few become truly active sexually before adolescence. And when they do (for girls more often than boys), it is seldom immediately related to sexual feelings or gratifications but is a use of sex for nonsexual goals and purposes. The "seductive" Lolita is rare; but she is significant: She illustrates a more general pattern of psychosexual development—a commitment to the social relationships linked to sex before one can really grasp the social meaning of the physical relationships.

Of great importance are the values (or feelings, or images) that children pick up as being related to sex. Although we talk a lot about sexuality, as though trying to exorcise the demon of shame, learning about sex in our society is in large part learning about guilt; and learning how to manage sexuality commonly involves learning how to manage guilt. An important source of guilt in children comes from the imputation to them by adults of sexual appetites or abilities that they may not have, but that they learn, however imperfectly, to pretend they have. The gestural concomitants of sexual modesty are learned early. For instance, when do girls learn to sit or pick up objects with their knees together? When do they learn that the bust must be covered? However, since this behavior is learned unlinked to later adult sexual performances, what children must make of all this is very mysterious.

The learning of sex roles, or sex identities, involves many things that are remote from actual sexual experience, or that become involved with sexuality only after puberty. Masculinity or femininity, their meaning and postures, are rehearsed before adolescence in many nonsexual ways.

A number of scholars have pointed, for instance, to the importance of aggressive, deference, dependency, and dominance behavior in childhood. Jerome Kagan and Howard Moss have found that aggressive behavior in males and dependency in females are relatively stable aspects of development. But what is social role, and what is biology? They found that when aggressive behavior occurred among girls, it tended to appear most often among those from well-educated families that were more tolerant of deviation. Curiously, they also reported that "it was impossible to predict the character of adult sexuality in women from their preadolescent and early adolescent behavior," and that "erotic activity is more anxiety-arousing for females than for males," because "the traditional ego ideal for women dictates inhibition of sexual impulses."

The belief in the importance of early sex-role learning

for boys can be viewed in two ways. First, it may directly indicate an early sexual capacity in male children. Or, second, early masculine identification may merely be an appropriate framework within which the sexual impulse (salient with puberty) and the socially available sexual scripts (or accepted patterns of sexual behavior) can most conveniently find expression. Our bias, of course, is toward the second.

But, as Kagan and Moss also noted, the sex role learned by the child does not reliably predict how he will act sexually as an adult. This finding also can be interpreted in the same two alternative ways. Where sexuality is viewed as a biological constant which struggles to express itself, the female sex role learning can be interpreted as the successful repression of sexual impulses. The other interpretation suggests that the difference lies not in learning how to handle a pre-existent sexuality, but in learning how to *be* sexual. Differences between men and women, therefore, will have consequences both for *what* is done sexually, as well as *when*.

Once again, we prefer the latter interpretation, and some recent work that we have done with lesbians supports it. We observed that many of the major elements of their sex lives—the start of actual genital sexual behavior, the onset and frequency of masturbation, the time of entry in sociosexual patterns, the number of partners, and the reports of feelings of sexual deprivation—were for these homosexual women almost identical with those of ordinary women. Since sexuality would seem to be more important for lesbians—after all, they sacrifice much in order to follow their own sexual pathways—this is surprising. We concluded that the primary factor was something both categories of women share—the sex-role learning that occurs before sexuality itself becomes significant.

Social class also appears significant, more for boys than girls. Sex-role learning may vary by class; lower-class boys are supposed to be more aggressive and put much greater emphasis on early heterosexuality. The middle and upper classes tend to tolerate more deviance from traditional attitudes regarding appropriate male sex-role performances.

Given all these circumstances, it seems rather naive to think of sexuality as a constant pressure, with a peculiar necessity all its own. For us, the crucial period of childhood has significance not because of sexual occurrences, but because of nonsexual developments that will provide the names and judgments for later encounters with sexuality.

The actual beginnings and endings of adolescence are vague. Generally, the beginning marks the first time society, as such, acknowledges that the individual has sexual capacity. Training in the postures and rhetoric of the sexual experience is now accelerated. Most important, the adolescent begins to regard those about him (particularly his peers, but also adults) as sexual actors and finds confirmation from others for this view.

For some, as noted, adolescent sexual experience begins before they are considered adolescents. Kinsey reports that a tenth of his female sample and a fifth of his male sample had experienced orgasm through masturbation by age 12. But still, for the vast majority, despite some casual play and exploration that post-Freudians might view as masked sexuality, sexual experience begins with adolescence. Even those who have had prior experience find that it acquires new meanings with adolescence. They now relate such meanings to both larger spheres of social life and greater senses of self. For example, it is not uncommon during the transition between childhood and adolescence for boys and, more rarely, girls to report arousal and orgasm while doing things not manifestly sexual—climbing trees, sliding down bannisters, or other activities that involve genital contact—without defining them as sexual. Often they do not even take it seriously enough to try to explore or repeat what was, in all likelihood, a pleasurable experience.

Adolescent sexual development, therefore, really represents the beginning of adult sexuality. It marks a definite break with what went on before. Not only will future experiences occur in new and more complex contexts, but they will be conceived of as explicitly sexual and thereby begin to complicate social relationships. The need to manage sexuality will rise not only from physical needs and desires, but also from the new implications of personal relationships. Playing, or associating, with members of the opposite sex now acquires different meanings.

At adolescence, changes in the developments of boys and girls diverge and must be considered separately. The one thing both share at this point is a reinforcement of their new status by a dramatic biological event—for girls, menstruation, and for boys, the discovery of the ability to ejaculate. But here they part. For boys, the beginning of a commitment to sexuality is primarily genital; within two years of puberty all but a relatively few have had the experience of orgasm, almost universally brought about by masturbation. The corresponding organizing event for girls is not genitally sexual but social: they have arrived at an age where they will learn role performances linked with proximity to marriage. In contrast to boys, only two-thirds of girls will report ever having masturbated (and, characteristically, the frequency is much less). For women, it is not until the late twenties that the incidence of orgasm from any source reaches that of boys at age 16. In fact, significantly, about half of the females who masturbate do so only after having experienced orgasm in some situation involving others. This contrast points to a basic distinction between the developmental processes for males and females: males move from privatized personal sexuality to sociosexuality; females do the reverse and at a later stage in the life cycle.

We have worked hard to demonstrate the dominance of social, psychological, and cultural influences over the biological; now, dealing with adolescent boys, we must briefly reverse course. There is much evidence that the early male

sexual impulses—again, initially through masturbation—
are linked to physiological changes, to high hormonal inputs
during puberty. This produces an organism that, to put it
simply, is more easily turned on. Male adolescents report
frequent erections, often without apparent stimulation of
any kind. Even so, though there is greater biological sensitization and hence masturbation is more likely, the meaning, organization, and continuance of this activity still
tends to be subordinate to social and psychological factors.

Masturbation provokes guilt and anxiety among most
adolescent boys. This is not likely to change in spite of
more "enlightened" rhetoric and discourse on the subject
(generally, we have shifted from stark warnings of mental,
moral, and physical damage to vague counsels against non-
social or "inappropriate" behavior). However, it may be
that this very guilt and anxiety gives the sexual experience
an intensity of feeling that is often attributed to sex itself.

Such guilt and anxiety do not follow simply from social
disapproval. Rather, they seem to come from several sources,
including the difficulty the boy has in presenting himself
as a sexual being to his immediate family, particularly his
parents. Another source is the fantasies or plans associated
with masturbation—fantasies about doing sexual "things"
to others or having others do sexual "things" to oneself;
or having to learn and rehearse available but proscribed
sexual scripts or patterns of behavior. And, of course, some
guilt and anxiety center around the general disapproval
of masturbation. After the early period of adolescence, in
fact, most youths will not admit to their peers that they
did or do it.

Nevertheless, masturbation is for most adolescent boys
the major sexual activity, and they engage in it fairly frequently. It is an extremely positive and gratifying experience to them. Such an introduction to sexuality can lead
to a capacity for detached sex activity—activity whose only
sustaining motive is sexual. This may be the hallmark of
male sexuality in our society.

Of the three sources of guilt and anxiety mentioned, the first—how to manage both sexuality and an attachment to family members—probably cuts across class lines. But the others should show remarkable class differences. The second one, how to manage a fairly elaborate and exotic fantasy life during masturbation, should be confined most typically to the higher classes, who are more experienced and adept at dealing with symbols. (It is possible, in fact, that this behavior, which girls rarely engage in, plays a role in the processes by which middle-class boys catch up with girls in measures of achievement and creativity and, by the end of adolescence, move out in front. However, this is only a hypothesis.)

The ability to fantasize during masturbation implies certain broad consequences. One is a tendency to see large parts of the environment in an erotic light, as well as the ability to respond, sexually and perhaps poetically, to many visual and auditory stimuli. We might also expect both a capacity and need for fairly elaborate forms of sexual activity. Further, since masturbatory fantasies generally deal with relationships and acts leading to coitus, they should also reinforce a developing capacity for heterosociality.

The third source of guilt and anxiety—the alleged "unmanliness" of masturbation—should more directly concern the lower-class male adolescent. ("Manliness" has always been an important value for lower-class males.) In these groups, social life is more often segregated by sex, and there are, generally, fewer rewarding social experiences from other sources. The adolescent therefore moves into heterosexual—if not heterosocial—relationships sooner than his middle-class counterparts. Sexual segregation makes it easier for him than for the middle-class boy to learn that he does not have to love everything he desires, and therefore to come more naturally to casual, if not exploitative, relationships. The second condition—fewer social rewards that his fellows would respect—should lead to an exaggerated concern for proving masculinity by direct displays of physical prowess, aggression, and visible sexual success. And these three, of course, may be mutually reinforcing.

In a sense, the lower-class male is the first to reach "sexual maturity" as defined by the Freudians. That is, he is generally the first to become aggressively heterosexual and exclusively genital. This characteristic, in fact, is a distinguishing difference between lower-class males and those above them socially.

But one consequence is that although their sex lives are almost exclusively heterosexual, they remain homosocial. They have intercourse with females, but the standards and the audience they refer to are those of their male fellows.

Middle-class boys shift predominantly to coitus at a significantly later time. They, too, need and tend to have homosocial elements in their sexual lives. But their fantasies, their ability to symbolize, and their social training in a world in which distinctions between masculinity and femininity are less sharply drawn, allow them to withdraw more easily from an all-male world. This difference between social classes obviously has important consequences for stable adult relationships.

One thing common in male experience during adolescence is that while it provides much opportunity for sexual commitment, in one form or another, there is little training in how to handle emotional relations with girls. The imagery and rhetoric of romantic love is all around us; we are immersed in it. But whereas much is undoubtedly absorbed by the adolescent, he is not likely to tie it closely to his sexuality. In fact, such a connection might be inhibiting, as indicated by the survival of the "bad-girl-who-does" and "good-girl-who-doesn't" distinction. This is important to keep in mind as we turn to the female side of the story.

In contrast to males, female sexual development during adolescence is so similar in all classes that it is easy to suspect that it is solely determined by biology. But, while girls do not have the same level of hormonal sensitization to sexuality at puberty as adolescent boys, there is little evidence of a biological or social inhibitor either. The "equipment" for sexual pleasure is clearly present by puberty, but tends not to be used by many females of any class. Masturbation rates are fairly low, and among those who do masturbate, fairly infrequent. Arousal from "sexual" materials or situations happens seldom, and exceedingly few girls report feeling sexually deprived during adolescence.

Basically, girls in our society are not encouraged to be sexual—and may be strongly discouraged from being so. Most of us accept the fact that while "bad boy" can mean many things, "bad girl" almost exclusively implies sexual delinquency. It is both difficult and dangerous for an adolescent girl to become too active sexually. As Joseph Rheingold puts it, where men need only fear sexual failure, women must fear both success and failure.

Does this long period of relative sexual inactivity among girls come from repression of an elemental drive, or merely from a failure to learn how to be sexual? The answers have important implications for their later sexual development. If it is repression, the path to a fuller sexuality must pass through processes of loss of inhibitions, during which the girl unlearns, in varying degrees, attitudes and values that block the expression of natural internal feelings. It also implies that the quest for ways to express directly sexual behavior and feelings that had been expressed nonsexually is secondary and of considerably less significance.

On the other hand, the "learning" answer suggests that women create or invent a capacity for sexual behavior, learning how and when to be aroused and how and when to respond. This approach implies greater flexibility; unlike the repression view, it makes sexuality both more and less than a basic force that may break loose at any time in strange or costly ways. The learning approach also lessens the power of sexuality altogether; all at once, particular kinds of sex activities need no longer be defined as either "healthy" or "sick." Lastly, subjectively, this approach appeals to the authors because it describes female sexuality in terms that seem less like a mere projection of male sexuality.

If sexual activity by adolescent girls assumes less specific forms than with boys, that does not mean that sexual learning and training do not occur. Curiously, though girls are, as a group, far less active sexually than boys, they receive far more training in self-consciously viewing themselves—and in viewing boys—as desirable mates. This is particularly true in recent years. Females begin early in adolescence to define attractiveness, at least partially, in sexual terms. We suspect that the use of sexual attractiveness for nonsexual purposes that marked our preadolescent "seductress" now begins to characterize many girls. Talcott Parsons' description of how the wife "uses" sex to bind the husband to the family, although harsh, may be quite accurate. More generally, in keeping with the childbearing and child-raising function of women, the development of a sexual role seems to involve a need to include in that role more than pleasure.

To round out the picture of the difference between the sexes, girls appear to be well-trained precisely in that area in which boys are poorly trained—that is, a belief in and a capacity for intense, emotionally-charged relationships and the language of romantic love. When girls during this period describe having been aroused sexually, they more often report it as a response to romantic, rather than erotic, words and actions.

In later adolescence, as dates, parties, and other sociosexual activities increase, boys—committed to sexuality and relatively untrained in the language and actions of romantic love—interact with girls, committed to romantic love and relatively untrained in sexuality. Dating and courtship may well be considered processes in which each sex trains the other in what each wants and expects. What data is available suggests that this exchange system does not always work very smoothly. Thus, ironically, it is not uncommon to find that the boy becomes emotionally involved with his partner and therefore lets up on trying to seduce her, at the same time that the girl comes to feel that the boy's affection is genuine and therefore that sexual intimacy is more permissible.

In our recent study of college students, we found that boys typically had intercourse with their first coital partners one to three times, while with girls it was ten or more. Clearly, for the majority of females first intercourse becomes possible only in stable relationships or in those with strong bonds.

The male experience does conform to the general Freudian expectation that there is a developmental movement from a predominantly genital sexual commitment to a loving relationship with another person. But this movement is, in effect, reversed for females, with love or affection often a necessary precondition for intercourse. No wonder, therefore, that Freud had great difficulty understanding female sexuality—recall the concluding line in his great essay on women: "Woman, what does she want?" This "error"—the assumption that female sexuality is similar to or a mirror image of that of the male—may come from the fact that so many of those who constructed the theory were men. With Freud, in addition, we must remember the very concept of sexuality essential to most of nineteenth century Europe—it was an elemental beast that had to be curbed.

It has been noted that there are very few class differences in sexuality among females, far fewer than among males. One difference, however, is very relevant to this discussion—the age of first intercourse. This varies inversely with social class—that is, the higher the class, the later the age of first intercourse—a relationship that is also true of first marriage. The correlation between these two ages suggest the necessary social and emotional linkage between courtship and the entrance into sexual activity on the part of women. A second difference, perhaps only indirectly related to social class, has to do with educational achievement: here, a sharp border line seems to separate from all other women those who have or have had graduate or professional work. If sexual success may be measured by the percentage of sex acts that culminate in orgasm, graduate and professional women are the most sexually successful women in the nation.

Why? One possible interpretation derives from the work of Abraham Maslow: Women who get so far in higher education are more likely to be more aggressive, perhaps to have strong needs to dominate; both these characteristics are associated with heightened sexuality. Another, more general interpretation would be that in a society in which girls are expected primarily to become wives and mothers, going on to graduate school represents a kind of deviancy —a failure of, or alienation from, normal female social adjustment. In effect, then, it would be this flawed socialization—not biology—that produced both commitment toward advanced training and toward heightened sexuality.

For both males and females, increasingly greater involvement in the social aspects of sexuality—"socializing" with the opposite sex—may be one factor that marks the end of adolescence. We know little about this transition, especially among noncollege boys and girls; but our present feeling is that sexuality plays an important role in it. First, sociosexuality is important in family formation and also in learning the roles and obligations involved in being an adult. Second, and more fundamental, late adolescence is when a youth is seeking, and experimenting toward finding, his identity—who and what he is and will be; and sociosexual activity is the one aspect of this exploration that we associate particularly with late adolescence.

Young people are particularly vulnerable at this time. This may be partly due to the fact that society has difficulty protecting the adolescent from the consequences of sexual behavior that it pretends he is not engaged in. But,

more importantly, it may be because, at all ages, we all
have great problems in discussing our sexual feelings and
experiences in personal terms. These, in turn, make it extremely difficult to get support from others for an adolescent's experiments toward trying to invent his sexual self.
We suspect that success or failure in the discovery or
management of sexual identity may have consequences in
personal development far beyond merely the sexual sphere
—perhaps in confidence and feelings of self-worth, belonging, competence, guilt, force of personality, and so on.

In our society, all but a few ultimately marry. Handling
sexual commitments inside marriage makes up the larger
part of adult experience. Again, we have too little data
for firm findings. The data we do have come largely from
studies of broken and troubled marriages, and we do not
know to what extent sexual problems in such marriages
exceed those of intact marriages. It is possible that, because we have assumed that sex is important in most
people's lives, we have exaggerated its importance in holding marriages together. Also, it is quite possible that, once
people are married, sexuality declines relatively, becoming
less important than other gratifications (such as domesticity
or parenthood) ; or it may be that these other gratifications
can minimize the effect of sexual dissatisfaction. Further,
it may be possible that individuals learn to get sexual
gratification, or an equivalent, from activities that are nonsexual, or only partially sexual.

The sexual desires and commitments of males are the
main determinants of the rate of sexual activity in our
society. Men are most interested in intercourse in the early
years of marriage—woman's interest peaks much later;
nonetheless, coital rates decline steadily throughout marriage. This decline derives from many things, only one
of which is decline in biological capacity. With many
men, it is more difficult to relate sexually to a wife who
is pregnant or a mother. Lower-class adult men receive
less support and plaudits from their male friends for

married sexual performance than they did as single adolescents; and we might also add the lower-class disadvantage of less training in the use of auxiliary or symbolic sexually stimulating materials. For middle-class men, the decline is not as steep, owing perhaps to their greater ability to find stimulation from auxiliary sources, such as literature, movies, music, and romantic or erotic conversation. It should be further noted that for about 30 percent of college-educated men, masturbation continues regularly during marriage, even when the wife is available. An additional (if unknown) proportion do not physically masturbate, but derive additional excitement from the fantasies that accompany intercourse.

But even middle-class sexual activity declines more rapidly than bodily changes can account for. Perhaps the ways males learn to be sexual in our society make it very difficult to keep it up at a high level with the same woman for a long time. However, this may not be vital in maintaining the family, or even in the man's personal sense of well-being, because, as previously suggested, sexual dissatisfaction may become less important as other satisfactions increase. Therefore, it need seldom result in crisis.

About half of all married men and a quarter of all married women will have intercourse outside of marriage at one time or another. For women, infidelity seems to have been on the increase since the turn of the century— at the same time that their rates of orgasm have been increasing. It is possible that the very nature of female sexuality is changing. Work being done now may give us new light on this. For men, there are strong social-class differences—the lower class accounts for most extramarital activity, especially during the early years of marriage. We have observed that it is difficult for a lower-class man to acquire the appreciation of his fellows for married intercourse; extramarital sex, of course, is another matter.

In general, we feel that far from sexual needs affecting

other adult concerns, the reverse may be true: adult sexual activity may become that aspect of a person's life most often used to act out other needs. There are some data that suggest this. Men who have trouble handling authority relationships at work more often have dreams about homosexuality; some others, under heavy stress on the job, have been shown to have more frequent episodic homosexual experiences. Such phenomena as the rise of sadomasochistic practices and experiments in group sex may also be tied to nonsexual tensions, the use of sex for nonsexual purposes.

It is only fairly recently in the history of man that he has been able to begin to understand that his own time and place do not embody some eternal principle or necessity, but are only dots on a continuum. It is difficult for many to believe that man can change, and is changing, in important ways. This conservative view is evident even in contemporary behavioral science; and a conception of man as having relatively constant sexual needs has become part of it. In an ever-changing world, it is perhaps comforting to think that man's sexuality does not change very much, and therefore is relatively easily explained. We cannot accept this. Instead, we have attempted to offer a description of sexual development as a variable social invention—an invention that in itself explains little, and requires much continuing explanation.

March 1969

How and Why
America's Sex Standards
Are Changing

IRA L. REISS

The popular notion that America is undergoing a
sexual "revolution" is a myth. The belief that our
more permissive sexual code is a sign of a general
breakdown of morality is also a myth. These two
myths have arisen in part because we have so little
reliable information about American sexual behavior.
The enormous public interest in sex seems to have
been matched by moralizing and reticence in scholarly
research—a situation that has only recently begun to
be corrected.

What *has* been happening recently is that our young
people have been assuming more responsibility for
their own sexual standards and behavior. The influence
of their parents has been progressively declining. The
greater independence given to the young has long
been evident in other fields—employment, spending,
and prestige, to name three. The parallel change in

sexual-behavior patterns would have been evident if similar research had been made in this area. One also could have foreseen that those groups least subject to the demands of old orthodoxies, like religion, would emerge as the most sexually permissive of all—men in general, liberals, non-churchgoers, Negroes, the highly educated.

In short, today's more permissive sexual standards represent not revolution but evolution, not anomie but normality.

My own research into current sexual behavior was directed primarily to the question, Why are some groups of people more sexually permissive than other groups? My study involved a representative sample of about 1500 people, 21 and older, from all over the country; and about 1200 high-school and college students, 16 to 22 years old, from three different states. On the pages that follow, I will first discuss some of the more important of my findings; then suggest seven general propositions that can be induced from these findings; and, finally, present a comprehensive theory about modern American sexual behavior.

A good many sociologists believe that most of the real differences between Negroes and whites are class differences—that if Negroes and whites from the same class were compared, any apparent differences would vanish. Thus, some critics of the Moynihan Report accused Daniel P. Moynihan of ignoring how much lower-class whites may resemble lower-class Negroes.

But my findings show that there are large variations in the way whites and Negroes *of precisely the same class* view premarital sexual permissiveness. Among the poor, for instance, only 32 percent of white males approve of intercourse before marriage under some circumstances—compared with 70 percent of Negro males. The variation is even more dramatic among lower-class females: 5 percent of whites compared with 33 percent of Negroes. Generally, high-school and college students of all classes were found to be more permissive than those in the adult sample. But even among students there were variations associated with race. (See Table I.)

TABLE I—Percent Accepting Premarital Sex

	Lower-class adults*	Lower-class students**
White men	32% of 202	56% of 96
Negro men	70% of 49	86% of 88
White women	5% of 221	17% of 109
Negro women	33% of 63	42% of 90

* From National Adult Sample
** From Five-School Student Sample

The difference between Negro and white acceptance of premarital intercourse is not due to any racial superiority or inferiority. All that this finding suggests is that we should be much more subtle in studying Negro-white differences, and not assume that variations in education, income, or occupation are enough to account for all these differences. The history of slavery, the depressing effects of discrimination and low status—all indicate that the Negro's entire cultural base may be different from the white's.

Another response to this finding on sexual attitudes can, of course, be disbelief. Do people really tell the truth about their sex lives? National studies have revealed that they do—women will actually talk more freely about their sex lives than about their husbands' incomes. And various validity checks indicate that they did in this case.

But people are not always consistent: They may not practice what they preach. So I decided to compare people's sexual attitudes with their actual sexual behavior. Table II indicates the degree of correspondence between attitudes and behavior in a sample of 248 unmarried, white, junior and senior college-students.

TABLE II—Sexual Standards and Actual Behavior

Current Standard	Most Extreme Current Behavior			Number of Respondents
	Kissing	Petting	Coitus	
Kissing	64%	32%	4%	25
Petting	15%	78%	7%	139
Coitus	5%	31%	64%	84

Obviously, the students do not *always* act as they believe. But in the great majority of cases belief and action do coincide. For example, 64 percent of those who consider coitus acceptable are actually having coitus; only 7 percent of those who accept nothing beyond petting, and 4 percent of those who accept nothing beyond kissing, are having coitus. So it is fairly safe to conclude that, in this case, attitudes are good clues to behavior.

What about guilt feelings? Don't they block any transition toward more permissive sexual attitudes and behavior? Here the findings are quite unexpected. *Guilt feelings do not generally inhibit sexual behavior.* Eighty-seven percent of the women and 58 percent of the men said they had eventually come to accept sexual activities that had once made them feel guilty. (Some—largely males—had never felt guilty.) Seventy-eight percent had *never* desisted from any sexual activity that had made them feel guilty. Typically, a person will feel some guilt about his sexual behavior, but will continue his conduct until the guilt diminishes. Then he will move on to more advanced behavior—and new guilt feelings—until over that; and so on. People differed, mainly, in the sexual behavior they were willing to start, and in how quickly they moved on to more advanced forms.

The factor that most decisively motivated women to engage in coitus and to approve of coitus was the belief that they were in love. Of those who accepted coitus, 78 percent said they had been in love—compared with 60 percent of those who accepted only petting, and 40 percent of those who accepted only kissing. (Thus, parents who don't want their children to have sexual experiences but do want them to have "love" experiences are indirectly encouraging what they are trying to prevent.)

How do parents' beliefs influence their children's sexual attitudes and conduct?

Curiously enough, almost two-thirds of the students felt that their sexual standards were at least similar to those of their parents. This was as true for Negro males as for white females—although about 80 percent of the former accept premarital intercourse as against only about 20 percent of the latter. Perhaps these students are deluded, but perhaps they see through the "chastity" facade of their parents to the underlying similarities in attitude. It may be that the parents' views on independence, love, pleasure, responsibility, deferred gratification, conformity, and adventurousness are linked with the sexual attitudes of their children; that a similarity in these values implies a similarity in sexual beliefs. Probably these parental values, like religiousness, help determine which youngsters move quickly and with relatively little guilt through the various stages of sexual behavior. Religiousness, for the group of white students, is a particularly good index: Youngsters who rank high on church attendance rank low on premarital coitus, and are generally conservative.

Despite the fact that 63 to 68 percent of the students felt that their sexual standards were close to their parents' standards, a larger percentage felt that their standards were even closer to those of peers (77 percent) and to those of very close friends (89 percent). Thus, the conflict in views between peers and parents is not so sharp as might be expected. Then too, perhaps parents' values have a greater influence on their children's choice of friends than we usually acknowledge.

This brings us to another key question. Are differences in sexual standards between parents and children due to changing cultural standards? Or are they due to their different roles in life—that is, to the difference between being young, and being parents responsible for the young? Were the parents of today that different when they courted?

My findings do show that older people tend to be less permissive about sex—but this difference is not very marked. What is significant is that childless couples— similar to couples with children of courtship age in every other respect, including age—are much more willing to accept premarital intercourse as standard (23 to 13 percent). Furthermore, parents tend to be *less* sexually permissive the *more* responsibility they have for young people. Now, if the primary cause of parent-child divergences in sexual standards is that cultural standards in general have been changing, then older people should, by and large, be strikingly more conservative about sex. They aren't. But since parents are more conservative about sex than nonparents of the same age, it would seem that the primary cause of parent-child divergences over sex is role and responsibility—the parents of today were *not* that different when courting.

Being responsible for others, incidentally, inhibits permissiveness even when the dependents are siblings. The first-born are far less likely to approve of premarital intercourse (39 percent) than are the youngest children (58 percent).

Another intriguing question is, How do parents feel about the sexual activities of their boy children—as opposed to their girl children? The answer depends upon the sex of the parent. The more daughters a white father has, the more strongly he feels about his standards—although his standards are no stricter than average. The more sons he has, the less strongly he feels about his beliefs. White mothers showed the reverse tendency, but much more weakly—the more sons, the stronger the mothers' insistence upon whatever standards they believed in. Perhaps white parents feel this way because of their unfamiliarity with the special sexual problems of a child of the opposite sex—combined with an increasing awareness of these problems.

What explains these differences in attitude between groups—differences between men and women as well as between Negroes and whites? Women are more committed to marriage than men, so girls become more committed to marriage too, and to low-permissive parental values. The economic pressures on Negroes work to break up their families, and weaken commitment to marital values, so Negroes tend to be more permissive. Then too, whites have a greater stake in the orthodox institution of marriage: More white married people than unmarried people reported that they were happy. Among Negroes, the pattern was reversed. But in discussing weak commitments to marriage we are dealing with one of the "older" sources of sexual permissiveness.

The sources of the new American permissiveness are somewhat different. They include access to contraception; ways to combat venereal infection; and—quite as important—an intellectualized philosophy about the desirability of sex accompanying affection. "Respectable," college-educated people have integrated this new philosophy with their generally liberal attitudes about the family, politics, and religion. And this represents a new and more lasting support for sexual permissiveness, since it is based on a positive philosophy rather than hedonism, despair, or desperation.

In my own study, I found that among the more permissive groups were those in which the fathers were professional men. This finding is important: It shows that the upper segments of our society, like the lower, have a highly permissive group in their midst—despite the neat picture described by some people of permissiveness steadily declining as one raises one's gaze toward the upper classes.

All these findings, though seemingly diverse, actually fall into definite patterns, or clusters of relationships. These patterns can be expressed in seven basic propositions:

The *less* sexually permissive a group is, traditionally, the *greater* the likelihood that new social forces will cause its members to become more permissive.

Traditionally high-permissive groups, such as Negro men, were the least likely to have their sexual standards changed by social forces like church-attendance, love affairs, and romantic love. Traditionally low-permissive groups, such as white females, showed the greatest sensitivity to these social forces. In addition, the lower social classes are reported to have a tradition of greater sexual permissiveness, so the finding that their permissiveness is less sensitive to certain social forces also fits this proposition.

The more liberal the group, the more likely that social forces will help maintain high sexual permissiveness.

There was diverse support for this proposition. Students, upper-class females in liberal settings, and urban dwellers have by and large accepted more permissiveness than those in more conservative settings.

Indeed, liberalism in general seems to be yet another cause of the new permissiveness in America. Thus, a group that was traditionally low-permissive regarding sex (the upper class), but that is liberal in such fields as religion and politics, would be very likely to shift toward greater premarital permissiveness.

According to their ties to marital and family insitutions, people will differ in their sensitivity to social forces that affect permissiveness.

This proposition emphasizes, mainly, male-female differences in courting. Women have a stronger attachment to and investment in marriage, childbearing, and family ties. This affects their courtship roles. There are fundamental male-female differences in acceptance of permissiveness, therefore, in line with differences in courtship role.

Romantic love led more women than men to become permissive (this finding was particularly true if the woman was a faithful churchgoer). Having a steady date affected women predominantly, and exclusiveness was linked with permissiveness. Early dating, and its link with permissiveness, varied by race, but was far more commonly linked with permissiveness in men than in women. The number of steadies, and the number of times in love, was associated with permissiveness for females, but was curvilinear for males—that is, a man with no steadies, or a number of steadies, tended to be more permissive than a man who had gone steady only once.

Such male-female differences, however, are significant only for whites. Among Negroes, male-female patterns in these areas are quite similar.

The higher the overall level of permissiveness in a group, the greater the extent of equalitarianism within abstinence and double-standard subgroups.

Permissiveness is a measure not only of what a person will accept for himself and his own sex, but of what behavior he is willing to allow the opposite sex. Permissiveness, I found, tends to be associated with sexual equalitarianism in one particular fashion: I found, strangely enough, that a good way to measure the *general* permissiveness of a group is to measure the equalitarianism of two subgroups—the abstinent, and believers in the double-standard. (Nonequalitarianism in abstinence means, usually, petting is acceptable for men, but only kissing for women. Equalitarianism within the double-standard means that intercourse is acceptable for women when in love, for men anytime. The nonequalitarian double-standard considers all unmarried women's coitus wrong.) In a generally high-permissive group (such as men), those adherents who do accept abstinence or the double-standard will be more equalitarian than will their counterparts in low-permissive groups (such as women). The implication is that the ethos of a high-permissive group encourages female sexuality and thereby also encourages equalitarianism throughout the group.

The potential for permissiveness derived from parents' values is a key determinant as to how rapidly, how much, and in what direction a person's premarital sexual standards and behavior change.

What distinguishes an individual's sexual behavior is not its starting point—white college-educated females, for instance, almost always start only with kissing—but how far, how fast, and in what direction the individual is willing to go. The fact is that almost all sexual behavior is eventually repeated, and comes to be accepted. And a person's basic values encourage or discourage his willingness to try something new and possibly guilt-producing. Therefore, these basic values—derived, in large part, from parental teaching, direct or implicit—are keys to permissiveness.

Since the young often feel that their sex standards are similar to their parents', we can conclude that, consciously or not, high-permissive parents intellectually and emotionally breed high-permissive children.

A youth tends to see permissiveness as a continuous scale with his parents' standards at the low point, his peers' at the high point, and himself between but closer to his peers—and closest to those he considers his most intimate friends.

The findings indicate that those who consider their standards closer to parents' than to peers' are less permissive than the others. The most permissive within one group generally reported the greatest distance from parents, and greatest similarity to peers and friends. This does not contradict the previous proposition, since parents are on the continuum and exert enough influence so that their children don't go all the way to the opposite end. But it does indicate, and the data bear out, that parents are associated with relatively low permissiveness; that the courtship group is associated with relatively high permissiveness; and that the respondents felt closer to the latter. Older, more permissive students were less likely to give "parental guidance" as a reason for their standards.

Greater responsibility for other members of the family, and lesser participation in courtship, are both associated with low-permissiveness.

The only child, it was found, had the most permissive attitudes. Older children, generally, were less permissive than their younger brothers and sisters. The older children usually have greater responsibility for the young siblings; children without siblings have no such responsibilities at all.

The findings also showed that as the number of children, and their ages, increased, the parents' permissiveness decreased. Here again, apparently, parental responsibility grew, and the decline in permissiveness supports the proposition above.

On the other hand, as a young person gets more and more caught up in courtship, he is progressively freed from parental domination. He has less responsibility for others, and he becomes more permissive. The fact that students are more sexually liberal than many other groups must be due partly to their involvement in courtship, and to their distance from the family.

Thus a generational clash of some sort is almost inevitable. When children reach their late teens or early 20s, they also reach the peak of their permissiveness; their parents, at the same time, reach the nadir of theirs.

These findings show that both the family and courtship institutions are key determinants of whether a person accepts or rejects premarital sexuality. Even when young people have almost full independence in courtship, as they do in our system, they do not copulate at random. They display parental and family values by the association of sex with affection, by choice of partners, by equalitarianism, and so on.

However, parental influence must inevitably, to some extent, conflict with the pressures of courting, and the standards of the courting group. Young people are tempted by close association with attractive members of the opposite sex, usually without having any regular heterosexual outlet. Also, youth is a time for taking risks and having adventures. Therefore, the greater the freedom to react autonomously within the courtship group, the greater the tendency toward liberalized sexual behavior.

This autonomy has always been strong in America. Visitors in the 19th century were amazed at freedom of mate choice here, and the equalitarianism between sexes, at least as compared with Europe. The trend has grown.

Now, families are oriented toward the bearing and rearing of children—and for this, premarital sex is largely irrelevant. It becomes relevant only if it encourages marriages the parents want—but relevant negatively if it encourages births out of wedlock, or the "wrong," or no, marriages. Most societies tolerate intercourse between an engaged couple, for this doesn't seriously threaten the marital institution; and even prostitution gains some acceptance because it does not promote unacceptable marital unions. The conflict between the family and courtship systems depends on the extent to which each perceives the other as threatening its interests. My own findings indicate that this conflict is present, but not always as sharply as the popular press would have us believe.

Courtship pressures tend toward high-permissiveness; family pressures toward low-permissiveness. It follows that whatever promotes the child's independence from the family promotes high-permissiveness. For example, independence is an important element in the liberal position; a liberal setting, therefore, generally encourages sexual as well as other independence.

To summarize all these findings into one comprehensive theory runs the risk of oversimplifying—if the findings and thought that went into the theory are not kept clearly in mind. With this *caveat,* I think a fair theoretical summary of the meaning of the foregoing material would be: How much premarital sexual permissiveness is considered acceptable in a courtship group varies directly with the independence of that group, and with the general permissiveness in the adult cultural environment.

In other words, when the social and cultural forces working on two groups are approximately the same, the differences in permissiveness are caused by differences in independence. But when independence is equal, differences come from differences in the socio-cultural setting.

There is, therefore, to repeat, no sexual revolution today. Increased premarital sexuality is not usually a result of breakdown of standards, but a particular, and different, type of organized system. To parents, more firmly identified with tradition—that is, with older systems—and with greater responsibilities toward the young, toward the family, and toward marriage, greater premarital sexuality seems deviant. But it is, nevertheless, an integral part of society—their society.

In short, there has been a gradually increasing acceptance of and overtness about sexuality. The basic change is toward greater equalitarianism, greater female acceptance of permissiveness, and more open discussion. In the next decade, we can expect a step-up in the pace of this change.

The greater change, actually, is in sexual attitude, rather than in behavior. If behavior has not altered in the last century as much as we might think, attitudes *have*—and attitudes and behavior seem closer today than for many generations. Judging by my findings, and the statements of my respondents, we can expect them to become closer still, and to proceed in tandem into a period of greater permissiveness, and even greater frankness. I do not, however, foresee extreme change in the years to come—such as full male-female equality. This is not possible unless male and female roles in the family are also equal, and men and women share equal responsibility for child-rearing and family support.

March 1968

FURTHER READING SUGGESTED BY THE AUTHOR:

The Encyclopedia of Sexual Behavior edited by Albert Ellis and Albert Albarbanel (New York City: Hawthorn Books, 1961). The most complete and authoritative source of its kind available. Contains articles by approximately 100 authorities in the field.

Hippie Morality- More Old Than New

BENNET M. BERGER

For a few months I've been going around the San Francisco Bay Area asking hippies what the New Morality is all about, and for more than a few months I've been reading and listening to their sympathizers and spokesmen, present and former: Paul Goodman, Edgar Friedenberg, Herbert Marcuse, Norman O. Brown, John Seeley, Alan Watts, Tim Leary, and Ken Kesey, among others. I read the *East Village Other* and the *Berkeley Barb,* and the *San Francisco Oracle* (when I can bear to), and I've been doing more than my share of cafe-sitting, digging the moral feeling of the young as it comes across through their talk. On the basis of this—forgive the expression—data, it would be very easy to argue (as I will) that there isn't much, if any, New Morality around, and certainly none that warrants upper-case letters (although how unprecedented or unheard of a morality must be to be regarded as "new" is a question too difficult for me to attempt to answer here).

But the conclusion that there isn't much new morality around is one I am reluctant to come to, because it almost inevitably functions as a put-down of various activities, some of which I actually want to encourage. Thus I am confronted with the very old problem of whether to speak the truth when it may have undesired consequences. To love the truth is no doubt a great virtue; but to love to speak the truth is a small vanity, and I should like to be very explicit that it is my vanity that constrains me to risk dampening the ardor of some of those who belong to a movement, which in many respects I admire, by attempting to speak the truth about it. People whose spirit may rest on an erroneous conviction that they are doing something new and revolutionary may be unhappy when told that they are (only) the most recent expression of what is by now an old tradition, even if it is, as I believe, an important and honorable tradition as well.

More than 30 years ago (a "generation," as Karl Mannheim reckoned social time, two generations as José Ortega y Gasset reckoned it, and three, four, or more as contemporary journalists and other grabbers of the main literary chance reckon it), the literary critic Malcolm Cowley wrote *Exile's Return,* a book about the experience of American literary expatriates in Europe in the 1920s. In it he treats to some extent the history of bohemianism, starting back in the middle of the 19th century with that important document of bohemian history, Henry Murger's *Scenes of Bohemian Life.* By 1920, Cowley says, bohemia had a relatively formal doctrine, "a system of ideas that could be roughly summarized as follows" (and as I go through these eight basic ideas, please keep in mind the hippies—and the fact that these ideas were formulated 33 years ago about phenomena that were then more than a hundred years old) :

■ The first point in the bohemian doctrine is what Cowley calls "The idea of salvation by the child.—Each of us at birth has special potentialities which are slowly crushed and destroyed by a standardized society and mechanical modes of teaching. If a new educational system can be introduced, one by which children are encouraged to develop their own personalities, to [listen!] blossom freely like flowers, then the world will be saved by this new, free generation." The analogues here are hippie innocence (more on this later), flower power, and the educational revolution.

■ "The idea of self-expression.—Each man's, each woman's, purpose in life is to express himself, to realize his full individuality through creative work and beautiful living in beautiful surroundings." This, I believe, is identical with the hippies' moral injunction to "do your thing."

■ "The idea of paganism.—The body is a temple in which there is nothing unclean, a shrine to be adorned for the ritual of love." Contemporary paganism, by no means limited to the hippies but especially prevalent among them, is manifest in the overpowering eroticism that their scene exudes: the prevalence of female flesh (toe, ankle, belly, breast, and thigh) and male symbols of strength (beards, boots, denim, buckles, motorcycles), or the gentler and more restrained versions of these, or the by-now hardly controversial assumption that fucking will help set you free.

■ "The idea of living for the moment.—It is stupid to pile up treasures that we can enjoy only in old age. . . . Better to seize the moment as it comes. . . . Better to live extravagantly . . . 'burn [your] candle at both ends. . . .' " Today, this might be formulated as something like being super WOW where the action is in the NOW generation, who, like, know what's happening and where it's at. (It was a gentle English cleric who said many years ago that the man who marries the spirit of his own age is likely to be a widower in the next. Prophets of rapid social change, please take notice.)

■ "The idea of liberty.—Every law . . . that prevents self-expression or the full enjoyment of the moment should be shattered and abolished. Puritanism is the great enemy." Today, this is manifest in the movement to legalize marihuana, to render ecstasy respectable (dancing in the park, orgiastic sex, turning everybody on, etc.), and to demonstrate the absurdity of laws against acts that harm no one and the hypocrisy of those who insist on the enforcement of these laws.

■ "The idea of female equality.—Women should be the economic and moral equals of men . . . same pay . . . same working conditions, the same opportunity for drinking, smoking, taking or dismissing lovers." For the hippies, insistence on equality in smoking and the taking and dismissing of lovers is already quaint, and drinking is increasingly irrelevant. But the theme of sexual equality is still important with respect to cultural differences between the sexes, and evident in the insistence that men may be gentle and women aggressive, and in the merging of sexually related symbols of adornment (long hair, beads, bells, colorful clothes, and so on).

■ Hippies often tell me that it is really quite difficult, if not impossible, to understand their scene without appreciating the importance of psychedelic drugs in it. Although I am inclined to believe this, the importance of mind-expansion in the bohemian doctrine was plain to Cowley 33 years ago. The references are dated but the main point of his seventh basic idea is unmistakable: "The idea of psychological adjustment.—We are unhappy because . . . we are repressed." To Cowley, the then-contemporary version of the doctrine prescribed that repression could and should be overcome by Freudian analysis, or by the mystic qualities of George Ivanovich Gurdjieff's psycho-physical disciplining, or by *a daily dose of thyroid*. Today, repression may be uptightness or "game reality," and it is not Freud but Reich, not thyroid but LSD, not Gurdjieff but yoga, I Ching, *The Book of the Dead,* or some other meditational means of transcending the realities that hang one up.

■ Cowley's final point in the bohemian doctrine is the old romantic love of the exotic. "The idea of changing place.— 'They do things better in . . .' " (you name it). At some times the wisdom of old cultures has been affirmed, at other times, wild and primitive places—anything that will break the puritan shackles. Paris, Mexico, Tahiti, Tangier, Big Sur. The contemporary hippie fascination with American Indians has a triple attraction: They were oppressed, they were nobly savage, and by a symbolic act of identification they became a part of one's American collective unconscious, reachable under the influence of drugs.

Hippie morality, then, at least that part of it perceivable from the outside, seems to be only the most recent expression of a long tradition. Having said this, I don't want to just leave it there, because if my saying that the morality isn't new functions as a put-down of what it actually is, then my statement is misleading. Let me try to clarify what I am getting at.

Some months ago I gave a talk on "black culture" to what I then mistakenly thought was the usual sort of polite, university-extension audience of culture-hungry schoolteachers and social workers—in this case, many of them Negro. I argued—tentatively, without much conviction, in the dispassionate style I have argued so far in this article—that although the idea of black culture seemed useful to me as a myth to bind Negroes together in a way that would enhance their ability to press their political demands, there seemed to be little in what the nationalists and other militants were touting as "black culture" that couldn't be understood as a combination of Southern regional patterns, evangelical Christianity, and lower-class patterns of the metropolitan ghetto. I had hardly finished when I found myself facing an angry and shouting group of people who felt they had been insulted, and who, in other circumstances, might simply have killed me as an enemy of the people (I am not being melodramatic). Later, it was pointed out to me that black culture was in the process of being formed, and if I didn't see it, that was because I didn't know where it was at (both of which may be true). Besides, my implying that there wasn't any was likely not only to weaken the myth but to impede the actual growth and development of the reality—which made me an enemy.

The logical form of this problem is an old one for sociologists who deal with issues of public resonance: the problem of self-fulfilling and self-denying assertions. So although I do not see among the hippies any system of values that warrants the pretentious solemnity of the phrase "New Morality," I believe that moralities old *and* new rise and fall in part through self-fulfilling and self-denying processes that may be activated by descriptive statements innocent of prescriptive intent. But knowing this destroys the possibility of innocence for those who make statements that affect outcomes they are interested in. There are, that is, always potentially ascendant, deviant, or subterranean moralities around, the numbers of whose adherents are subject to expansion or contraction partly on the basis of how persuasively the morality is talked up or down, glamorized or mystified, vitalized or stultified, and its prevalence exaggerated or minimized. Such processes affect the rigor with which sanctions are or are not applied, and therefore obstruct or facilitate not merely moral deviance but the prospect that deviance will become legitimate and proclaim its own propriety. Joseph Conrad, that famous Polish sociologist, used as an epigraph for his very sociological *Lord Jim* the following words: "It is certain that my conviction increases the moment another soul will believe it."

Hippie morality is not new, but I think that more souls are believing it. The proportions of the age-grade may not be any larger, but the absolute numbers are enormous— for two very good and rather new reasons. First, there is the unprecedented, colossal size of the cohort between, say, 13 and 25, even a small percentage of which produces very large numbers indeed. Second, this cohort of morally deviant youth has been further swelled by the group known as "teeny-boppers"—pre-adolescents and early adolescents who have not, to my knowledge, previously played any significant role in bohemian movements. Their presence on the contemporary scene is, I think, a function of the institutionalization of adolescence, not simply as the traditional "transitional stage," but as a major period of life. This period may last as long as 20 years, and therefore evokes its own orientational phenomena and behavior, which we have learned to understand as "anticipatory socialization."

In addition to the hippies' large numbers, their peculiar visibility is playing an important part in the gradual legitimation of their traditionally subterranean morality. Exactly *un*like Michael Harrington's invisible poor, the hippies are unequally distributed in ways that magnify their visibility. They are concentrated—segregated in universities, or recently out of them and into the bohemian ghettos of the more glamorous big cities. They are colorful, disturbing, and always newsworthy. Moreover, they have a substantial press of their own and radio stations that play their music almost exclusively. And not only are many of them the children of relatively affluent and influential people, but they have their sympathizers (secret and not so secret) in the universities, and let's not forget the ballet, and in the mass media.

How do I know the bohemian morality is gradually being legitimated? I don't for sure, but when John Lennon said the Beatles were more popular than Jesus—something that probably wasn't even quite true—he got away with it, *and helped make it truer by getting away with it.* There's better evidence. Take sex, which in this country seems to be the quintessence of morality. More important and more reliable than survey data reporting premarital sexual experience are the revealing attitudes of more or less official moral spokesmen. Hollywood films, for example, are as good an indicator of acceptable morality as one is likely to find (appealing, as their producers say they must, to mass sentiments), and these films not only affirm unmarried sex but even suggest that your life may be ruined by the decision *not* to climb into bed with the person you love. It is still news when Christian ministers refuse to condemn unchastity, but it makes the inside pages now, and it is not nearly so startling an event as it was a few years ago. And now, finally, the topic is ready for discussion in the public schools: *Is* premarital intercourse wrong? William Graham Sumner gave us the answer: The moment the mores are questioned, they have lost their authority. And when they are questioned publicly by official representatives of the major institutions, they not only have lost their authority but are ready to be replaced—not, let me repeat, by a "New Morality" but by an old one that has been underground, and that now, like Yeats' rough beast, its hour come round at last, slouches toward Bethlehem to be born.

So what else is new? Well, several things that express traditional bohemian virtues in so fresh, unusual, and potentially consequential a manner that they are worth noting.

■ A few words about hippie innocence. Clearly, the symbols of childhood and innocence are very much *in*: flowers, ice cream, kites, beads, bells, bubbles, and feathers, and sitting on the ground, like Indians, or legs outstretched in front of one, like Charlie Brown and his friends (perhaps reflecting the guilelessness of the prose styles of Paul Goodman and Alan Watts?). Just recently, hippie innocence was a major theme in a CBS documentary oddly titled "The Hippie Temptation." CBS (Harry Reasoner, that is) disapproved, pointing out that the innocence is used in a hostile way (a girl taunts an annoyed policeman by insistently offering him flowers), and concluding with the (smug?) observation that people who can grow beards and make love ought to go beyond innocence to wisdom. What CBS apparently chose to ignore (and I say "chose" because it seems so obvious) was the fact that innocence *as* wisdom and the child *as* moral leader are two ideas that go back a couple of thousand years to very respectable sources. Harry Reasoner, a man with a usually reliable sense of irony, also chose to ignore the irony of network TV prescribing wisdom—and to the "TV generation"! Of *course,* hippie innocence is provocative; it angers the police, it angers CBS, and it is potentially consequential because authority finds it difficult to fight. Wisdom might be a good antidote, but there's very little wisdom around (and more people pleading incompetence to preach it). There's only sophistication, and not too much of that.

■ Another interesting development in the hippie milieu

is the panhandling. It's interesting because of its relation to the innocence theme, and because of the peculiar moral relevance of the interaction. The approach is usually the standard "Do you have any spare change?" But it is often consciously winsome and "charming." A teen-age girl, for example, asks me to lend her 15 cents for an ice-cream cone, then asks for 2 cents more so she can have the ice cream in a sugar cone. The mood of the interaction is different from skid-row panhandling, where the bum plays humble and subservient, thus allowing his mark to feel generous or powerful—or even contemptuous—which is what the giver gets in return for giving. Hippie panhandling is inno-cent, offhand, as if to say "You've got it and can spare it, I haven't; all men are brothers, and if you don't give, you're a kind of fink; or, if you think it's principle that prevents you from giving, it reveals only your uptightness about money, your enslavement to an obsolete ethic about the virtue of *earning* what you get." Indeed, one of the things one may learn from being approached is the shock-ing discovery that one *does* truly believe in that virtue. Whatever the specific character of one's response, the peo-ple I have spoken to invariably find it obscurely disturb-ing, an occasion for reflection, and this is important.

■ The hippies have also played an important role in the gradual institutionalization of the use of formerly obscene and other taboo language in public, even on ceremonial occasions. This trend is part of the general eroticization of public life, from print, to advertising, to film, to styles of dress and undress, and it has within it the potential for changing the quality of public life through its effect on spoken rhetoric, which may help reclaim the language from the depths to which public speech has sunk it. Lenny Bruce was a prophet of this trend. The so-called filthy-speech movement at Berkeley in the summer of 1965 is well-known, and so are the rather severe sanctions invoked against the offenders. What is not so well-known is that, shortly after this controversy, the university sponsored a poetry conference on the campus. For almost a whole week, there were daily and nightly readings, by, among others, several of the more successful beat poets of the '50s, as well as by many very young and relatively unknown hippie poets. I remember sitting in the hallowed halls of Wheeler Auditorium and the only slightly less hallowed Dwinelle Hall, amidst little old ladies with knitting, suburban house-wives from Orinda, and cashmere-sweatered undergradu-ates holding tight to their boyfriends' hands. And I re-member listening to Allen Ginsberg rhapsodize about wak-ing up with his cock in the mouth of his friend Peter Or-lovsky; I remember listening to other poets wax eloquent about cunnilinctus and about what they repeatedly insisted upon calling "fucking." Now, because I am a sociologist as well as a person interested in poetry, I remember not only sitting and listening to the poets, but I also remember observing that the ladies hardly looked up from their knit-ting and the undergraduates listened raptly (with that almost oppressive quiet reminiscent of museums), and I heard neither a titter nor a gasp of shock. I saw no out-raged exits, and not an indignant word in the press that week about pornography or obscenity. Nor was I aware of any other complaints against the use of university facil-ities for such goings-on—although the organizer of the conference told me, when I spoke to him about it later, that there had been one or two letters of complaint. One or two. And, I must confess, it is the improbability of negative sanctions that encourages me, here, to contribute to the tendency I am describing, that is, to *show* you my point rather than argue it: that formerly taboo language is increasingly used in public, and that, yes, Virginia, it is erotic. Nor is the poetry conference the only example at hand. As Bay Area residents well know, Lenore Kandel's *The Love Book,* shortly after being banned by the San Francisco police, was read aloud at a mass meeting of faculty and students at San Francisco State. And I have been told by the cast of *The Beard*—a one-act play that had a long run in San Francisco before its New York opening, which uses all the four-letter words and winds up with an act of cunnilinctus on stage—that their performances on campuses before college groups have been invariably successful: The audiences laugh in the funny places, not in the dirty ones. Only the Saturday night audiences in their San Francisco theater still leave a good deal to be desired.

■ The music (rock, folk-rock, etc.), of course, is new, but I will not discuss it at any length except to point to some features of it that I think may have important social consequences. First of all, the lyrics of many of the songs are—for the first time in the history of popular music in this country—lyrics that a thoughtful person of some sensibility and taste can sing without embarrassment. Think of it! Intelligent people singing popular songs seriously! Cole Porter was an exception to the rule of banality. Bob Dylan is not an exception because there is no longer a rule. Dylan is no great poet; he's not even a very good one. But he *is* a poet in a country where lyricists have usually been versifiers rather than poets. Second, I am struck by the fact that few, if any, of the traditional popular baritones sing rock well, or sing good rock well, or sing rock at all. It seems apparent that rock songs are not made for deep or mature voices; there is a prevalence of high, reedy, thin, sometimes even falsetto male voices—indeed, when listening to rock songs, one often finds it difficult to tell the difference between a male and a female voice. Enunciation, when it can be understood at all, is often childlike, sometimes even infantile. Postures tend to be limp, and facial expressions unformed and vulnerable. All this tends to identify the music with an age-group and a life-style, a distinctive kind of music for a distinctive kind of people— music that outsiders may admire, if they do, only as a tourist admires an exotic scene, but closer intimacy with which exposes one to the dangers of infection by other aspects of the life-style. Finally, there is the fact that rock groups typically do their own material almost exclusively, something—as far as I know—unprecedented in American popular music. And even when a song is very successful, other groups do not generally perform it. This may well express the importance of the idea of authenticity in the subculture, that doing your thing should be doing *your* thing, which would discourage a rock group from doing something that wasn't "theirs."

It is, of course, easy to deflate the authenticity balloon by pointing out that certain "things" can be authentically evil, and that doing *your* thing can be indirectly damaging to lots of people, including yourself. Qualifications, then, are necessary, but they are not usually made by moralists; the great moral dicta are typically stated in absolute terms, and never with all of the qualifications necessary to live with them. The commandment prohibiting homicide does not, after all, say except in self-defense, or except at the order of the commander-in-chief; and we all know that we may be pardoned our inability to honor our mothers and fathers if they push heroin in the high-school cafeteria.

This brings me to the question of the value of the not-so-new hippie morality. Unfortunately, we sociologists are among those least likely to speak with sympathy about expressive morality, because, of all data, data on morality reveal the greatest disparity between the point of view of the participant and that of the observer. The participant sees consummation, whereas we observers typically treat expressive morality as social facts whose prime significance lies in the institutional functions they facilitate or obstruct. As sociologists, we avoid moral discourse and resist indulging our moral feelings—because our scientific education has taught us that all moralities are ultimately arbitrary, and as men of science we have learned to abhor arbitrariness. Moralists frequently embarrass or bore sociologists: Their moralists' passion keeps demanding a like response from us, whereas *our* impulse is to look only for latent functions. But, like Philoctetes, the moralist has a magic bow as well as a festering wound, for one of the important manifest functions of the moralist's passion is to define or affirm or redefine the standards with reference to which expressive satisfactions are achieved. And to the extent that scientists get expressive satisfactions through their work, these standards are never irrelevant.

The closest that sociologists usually get to real moral judgment is when they invoke comparative data as a source or norms to appraise morally relevant situations. This angers and frustrates moralists, because their mission is utopian. In moral discourse, reliance on norms of evaluation derived from comparative data leaves one impotent to affect the standards in terms of which the evaluations are made; it renders one morally acted upon rather than morally active. For moralists, the invocation of comparative norms is irrelevant. If the moralists appear fanatical, intransigent, and unreasonable, it is because they must believe that moral feeling is not negotiable, that half a consummation is no consummation at all. It makes no difference that Americans are freer than Peruvians or Iranians and more humane than Guatemalans or Guineans; in terms of some current moral vision of human possibility, America may still stink. Where expressive values rather than facts or judicious estimates are at stake, the utopian standard is more relevant than the comparative norm, and therefore sociologists make poor moral leaders. Let me conclude with an old Jewish joke that may clarify this somewhat. Jake says, "So nu, Sam, how's your wife?" And Sam says, "Compared to what?" It's funny because of the inappropriateness of the comparative norm. How, then, is the hippie morality? Compared to what? No worse than anybody else's, better than many, but still not good enough.

December 1967

The Horseless Cowboys

JOHN A. POPPLESTONE

Kid Sheleen is a character in a satirical Western movie called *Cat Ballou*. Sheleen (Lee Marvin's Academy Award role) has degenerated from his glorious days as a successful gunfighter. When the movie opens he's just an aging drunk, riding around on a drunken horse with his face unshaven and his clothes ragged and forlorn. But at the point in the picture when Sheleen desperately wants to assert his youth and masculinity—because he wants to win gorgeous Jane Fonda—he goes back to being a bold gunfighter and kills the villain.

His preparation for this act is a transformation scene that rivals the one in Cinderella. When Sheleen wants to be a man again, what he does is get dressed—very slowly and ceremonially—in the clothing that proclaims the Western hero. He shaves, hides his beer-paunch with a tight corset, puts on tight black cowboy pants, polished boots, neck scarf, Stetson hat, and ties on a pair of elaborate silver guns. The clothes are Sheleen's armor. When he's drunk and on the skids, he carries them around in a little trunk; whenever he puts them on again, his manhood is restored. Sheleen is a comic character, but the way he uses his clothes to reconstruct his manhood is not entirely a scriptwriter's invention. That Sheleen is a character in a Western doesn't detract from the reality of his behavior.

Americans are addicted to Westerns; we read Western novels, we watch Western TV shows, we see Western movies. The Western is the great American fantasy. The examination of a patient's fantasy—its repetitions, eliminations, exaggerations, the kinds of people in it—has for years been one of the psychotherapist's most useful tools. If the Western is a kind of mass American fantasy, then we ought to be able to find out quite a bit about what we Americans are like by examining this shared, repetitious, but apparently endlessly satisfying canned fantasy. Americans use their Western fantasy in three ways:

■ *The vicarious experience.* Many people are content for the space of a TV show or a movie, just to watch, to sympathize with the characters, to live in the world of the Western for an hour or so.

■ *The participant fantasy.* For others, vicarious experience is not enough. These are men who join fast-draw clubs or vacation on dude ranches.

■ *The exoskeletal defense.* These are Sheleen's spiritual kin—the men who identify themselves entirely with the Western hero by the simple expedient of wearing his clothes. The clothes form an external skeleton, a kind of armor against the world. They transform the average domesticated American into the prototypical Western hero—a tough, hard-riding, gun-toting figure exuding sex appeal.

"Exoskeleton" is a term taken from zoology. In that discipline the word means "a hard, supporting or protective structure developed on or secreted by the outside of the body, as the shell of a crustacean; the common type of skeleton in invertebrates." With very little change in meaning, the term can be taken over by psychology to mean the body covering a person chooses to support or protect his inner self. Perhaps the second part of the zoological definition fits psychologically too; and exoskeletal defense is chosen usually by people who feel threatened by the world around them, people who lack backbone.

There is no question that a great many American men, certainly not all cowpokes by occupation, do wear Western clothes. Such clothes—Levis or other tight fitting pants, high heeled boots, wide leather belts, fancy shirts, neck scarves, cowboy hats—are available in almost any department store in any part of the country and through mail order catalogues. Stores with names like the *Circle G Corral Shop*, the *Hitching Post, Chuck's Horseman's Rendezvous*, sell riding equipment and Western clothes in communities far, far from Texas. Levi Strauss, the oldest firm in the tight Western pants business, estimates that it sells from five to six million pairs a year. National distribution now is four times what it was in the prewar era, when Levis sold only in the western section of the country. One manufacturer of cowboy boots for the mass market makes 1,500,000 pairs a year for men, women, and children, and the market is getting better all the time. The boot industry projects an annual rise of 10 to 15 percent for the next decade.

What are the customers in this tremendous market actually buying? What self-image do the boots and the Levis conjure up for them? One way to find out is to show a group of people various bits of cowboy getup and see what associations they form. This was done with a group of 212 students in a college psychology course. The stimuli were pictures (shown above) of polished high-heeled boots, a pair of rough leather Wellington boots, a drawing of a man's legs (wearing Levis and seen from the back *a la* Marshal Dillon), and a heavily tooled leather belt with an Indian silver buckle. The pictures were shown for less than a minute each on closed-circuit TV, and the students were asked to write down "what the object suggested, what kind of person would wear it, or what it meant." The group put down a total of 668 associations; when these were classified by content, 330 were unequivocal references to the West or to the cowboy. Some of the symbols turned out to be more Western than others; the belt pulled 62 percent Western references, compared to a low of 28 percent for the Wellington boots. (The polished high-heeled boots elicited police or military references.)

From the associations it is clear that three different but overlapping Western traits were being described. First and most prominently, the Western hero is seen as the *masculine* prototype; the students called men who would wear such clothes "strong but kind," "adventurous," "rugged," "hearty," "athletic." The second characteristic is *aggressiveness;* men who wear these clothes are "rough and crude," "tough." The third characteristic is *erotic*—cowboys are sexy; the back view looked like "skin-tight Levis on a rope-swinging cowboy."

The essence of cowboy, then, is masculinity, aggressiveness, and sex. Certainly advertising copy writers are convinced that this is the image the cowboy projects. A cowboy hat, an ad says, has "two-fisted good looks." "Everything about a cowboy boot expresses masculinity." A "vaquero cardigan" has "the ruggedness of the old West" and "will get you more than admiration when you wear it." The aggressiveness inherent in the Western product can be so blatant as to be ostentatiously denied, as in an ad for a wide leather belt that began, "The Marquis de Sade was not necessarily the inspiration. . . ."

The erotic aspect of cowboyhood is prominent in the advertising world: a shirt is "tailored to fit close," blue jeans are praised for "snug-fitting crotch and tight-fitting legs," stretch denims are "real, he-man, Western-styled jeans you can train to shape to your form, dramatically different in fit and feel, the lo-rise, trim tapered lean lines enhance any figure."

A slightly different variety of sex appeal crops up in magazines written for male readers only. A recent one carried a series of 12 photographs, called "Cowboy at the Ranch," where the male model was wearing nothing but a cowboy hat or a pair of Western boots.

The kind of man who chooses exoskeletal defenses is the admakers' dream. He's the man who prefers to read appearances rather than essences, the man whose Western clothes make him aggressive and forbidding in a world that is always full of danger, the man who doubts his masculinity and gets the reassurance he needs from looking like a he-man. The advertising inducements fit this personality as closely as the Levis fit their wearer.

Western clothes, of course, are only one exoskeleton out of a whole closetful this personality may choose to wear. It may, for instance, decide to get tattooed. There is really very little doubt that tattoos are symbols of male toughness. When asked about the symbolism of tattooing, psychology students made very different interpretations of a TV image of an arm holding an ambiguous object, depending on whether the arm was tattooed or not. Without the tattoo, most subjects thought the arm belonged to an average kind of man, with a semi-skilled job, holding a piece of wood. But when the arm was emblazoned with a woman's face surrounded by flowers and a scroll with the name "Gladys," the arm was transformed—it seemed that of a "rugged and tough" man holding a broken bottle.

The exoskeletal references of tattoos (like those of cowboy boots) have been of great value to the advertising industry. The successful transformation of what had been a red-tipped cigarette with a very feminine image (Marlboro), into a product which men were willing to buy was accomplished by relentlessly presenting the cigarette as the kind a man with a tattoo would smoke. After the Marlboro campaign stopped using the tattooed hero, they have for several years now associated their product with a cowboy figure—so here we go again.

An exoskeleton is, of course, a kind of shell, and it's difficult to find out what's going on beneath it. Only intensive individual probing would reveal whether a man so armed against the world is freed from the rigid controls of his super-ego. For some practitioners of exoskeletal defense, being a make-believe cowboy may completely satisfy the need for violence and erotic exhibition. A man may behave like Casper Milquetoast, but he can feel that others see him as Marshal Dillon or even Jesse James.

May/June 1966

Our Unlovable Sex Laws

FRED RODELL

A rather ribald limerick has a last line that runs: "It's fun, but you know it's illegal." There could scarcely be a more precise summation of the gap between American sex practices and sex laws today. Kinsey and innumerable other less publicized investigators into the sexways of U.S. citizens have found that far more than a majority—perhaps as many as 90 percent of all U.S. adults—at some time in their lives take part in sexual activities from which, in Judge Morris Ploscowe's almost chaste phrase, they presumably "derive satisfaction" but which, under the law, amount to criminal acts. Although laws do vary from state to state, throughout most of the nation the only kinds of sexual gratification that are not potentially subject to police interference, arrest, even conviction, are three: petting or necking short of intercourse; solitary masturbation in private; and intercourse (in the orthodox manner) between husband and wife. And

even the latter may be illegal in Connecticut or Massachusetts if either married partner uses a contraceptive.

Merely to state these facts illumines their absurdity. It is
almost a certainty that most of the people who read these
words have committed—perhaps yesterday, perhaps years
ago—sex crimes of one sort or another: maybe fornication
(intercourse between two unmarried people of different sexes) ; maybe adultery (the same where one or both are
married but not to each other) ; maybe some mild and
youthful homosexual experience; maybe an unorthodox
form of sex behavior, probably oral or anal, with one's
own spouse. Not one in a million such episodes is likely
to be discovered, not one in a hundred million prosecuted.
While thousands of divorces are granted every year in New
York, where the sole ground for divorce is adultery, prosecution for adultery, a crime in New York, will not occur
once in a generation. Yet so long as laws against widespread sex practices remain on the books, however rarely
and gingerly enforced, police retain the right to spy and
reveal, political or personal enemies hold a handy wedge for
blackmail, and respect for all law sinks lower, as during
Prohibition days, due to the hypocrisy of such unenforced
and unenforceable bans on basically harmless sexual behavior.

Thanks in large part to the cheap and easy availability
of contraceptive devices, to the omnipresence of the auto-
mobile (for either transportation or stationary tryst), and
to more liberal community acceptance of conduct once considered beyond the pale, sexual freedom, on a private and
mutually consenting level, has steadily risen throughout

Ed. Note:

Since the publication of this article, the United States Supreme
Court has struck down Connecticut's anti-contraceptive statute in
Griswold v. *Connecticut* (1965) and has declared unconstitutional
all miscegenation laws in *Loving* v. *Virginia* (1967).

this century. The law, here often as archaic as it is usually impotent, has lagged farther and farther behind. One extreme example, recently in the news, involved a North Carolina statute under which a single homosexual act, even though committed in private, may be punished by imprisonment for sixty years. And this present provision is a relaxation of an older one whereby "the abominable and detestable crime against nature" might have brought a sentence of "death without the benefit of clergy."

As doctors, psychologists, sociologists, and plain observers of the sexual scene have long considered the laws against common, voluntary acts by adults more of a "crime against nature" than the acts themselves, so now the legal profession is belatedly making noises in the same direction. The U.S. Supreme Court, having finally agreed to review Connecticut's ridiculous ban on contraceptive advice (even by doctors), sales (even to married couples) and use (even by married couples), will undoubtedly declare it unconstitutional. Unconstitutional too, by several Supreme Court rulings in recent years, has been most censorship of allegedly obscene books, magazines, and motion pictures—such censorship being but an oblique legal repression of sexual expression. Most significantly, the reporters and advisors for the influential American Law Institute, in drawing up a model criminal code for the states, strongly urged, as the late Professor Fowler Harper, a pioneer in the field, recently put it, "that deviant sexual behavior between consenting adults, regardless of sex, should not constitute a criminal offense when carried on in privacy." And several states, led by Illinois, have begun to write this attitude into their laws.

Of course there are, at the other end of the scale, various forms of sex conduct that no one in his right mind would exempt from criminal penalties. Chief among these are the use of force or the threat of force to achieve sexual ends, most commonly rape, and the abuse or corruption of children by adults. Most people would also include, in this must-be-punished category, offensive sexual behavior performed in public and all forms of commercial sex or prostitution.

Yet even in the most abominated of these areas, common sense dictates a touch of caution about current laws. Thus, both rape and the abuse of minors are combined in the concept of statutory rape—or intercourse, however unforced or even invited, with a girl younger than the "age of consent." But the age of consent, varying in different states from as low as 14 to as high as 21, usually hovers around 16 or 18. This means that for almost every pregnant high-school girl (and their increasing numbers have been called a national scandal)—as well as for almost every unvirginal but more careful high-school girl—there is, technically, a rapist presumably at large. And should a college boy who uses the services of a hard-looking 17½-year-old prostitute —say in New York, where the age of consent is 18—be branded and punished as a rapist, as under present law?

Similarly, some of our laws making crimes of comparatively minor sex acts or gestures—because committed in public—may be too extreme and may also be discriminatory. Such laws directed against exhibitionists, voyeurs (or peeping Toms), and frotteurs (who rub against strangers in subways or other crowded places) are rarely applied to women, who may be just as guilty as men. As one lady lawyer, Harriet Pilpel, has gallantly pointed out, a man caught watching through a window while a woman undresses may be arrested as a voyeur, whereas if the sexes are reversed it is the undressing man who may be held as an exhibitionist. Likewise, laws against blatant public displays of homosexuality are almost always enforced only against men.

But where homosexuals ply their partner-seeking overtly

in public, the offensiveness may be no less than that of
street-walkers, even though money may not be its aim. As
for prostitution itself (along with its manservant, so to
speak, procuring) not without reason is it known as the
oldest profession. In no place and at no time in history have
laws prohibiting it proved effective, although regulation
and licensing have sometimes served to control it and so
diminish its more dangerous consequences, such as disease
and corruption of police.

In between laws of such anachronistic asininity, as those
that make crimes of simple fornication, adultery, or irregu-
lar man-and-wife bed behavior, and laws so essential to any
civilized society as those that penalize sex by violence or
the sexual mistreatment of youngsters, lies a vast and varied
jungle of sex legislation about much of which reasonable
men can and do differ. (Even the Supreme Court, liberal as
it has become of late, is rarely unanimous in censorship cases
where freedom of speech and press stand against suppression of published pornography, often run recklessly wild.)

It would be impossible, in a short space, to list all these
in-between sex laws which, in our current culture, may be
deemed dubious, unnecessary, or silly. They range from a
North Carolina statute prohibiting any "act of lewdness"
with a student "within three miles of a school or college"
(but, by negative implication, not if four miles away) to a
Vermont law that forbids the advertising of any drug as a
cure for venereal disease (which apparently lumps together
effective drugs and quack concoctions). Yet a few of these
laws deserve a word—because they are venerable, well-nigh
universal, and, as our sex habits and attitudes relax, increasingly controversial.

Although only two states completely outlaw birth-control
by mechanical means (other states regulate advertising and

place of sale of contraceptives), abortion—contraception's dangerous handmaiden and one of the nation's major socio-medical problems—is everywhere a crime which may be punished by as many as fifteen years in prison or, if the mother dies, even as murder. Most states make an exception if abortion is needed to save the mother's life, but not mere-ly to save her physical or mental health. Indeed, no state even legalizes an abortion because pregnancy was caused by rape. And the restrictions on legal abortions performed in hospitals by qualified doctors—usually disguised under a less ugly name as "d. and c." (dilation and curettage) — are stringent.

The well-known result of these rigid laws is the wide prevalence of illegal abortions performed in unsanitary sur-roundings by incompetent members of "abortion mills" for exorbitant fees—as well as the shockingly high proportion of deaths. Estimates of the number of illegal abortions per-formed in the U.S. run as high as a million a year, with not one in a thousand ever prosecuted. It is because of this al-most total breakdown in the effective enforcement of abor-tion laws—as well as for humanitarian reasons—that one of the proposals of the American Law Institute's model code would drastically relax present bans against legal abortions. And for those moralists who may fear that such relaxation would further encourage pre-marital or extra-marital sex, be aware that one expert has estimated that *90 percent of U.S. illegal abortions are performed on married women with three or more children,* which would put the number of unwed near-mothers seeking illegal relief from pregnancy well below 10 percent of the total.

Other sex crimes falling in the debatable zone, between forcible rape at one end and voluntary fornication at the other, include various so-called perversions of which ac-tive homosexuality is only one. As the statutes define them

—now precisely, now vaguely—they run a gamut from "carnal copulation with any beast" and "enticing to masturbation" to "lewd," "lascivious," or "unnatural" acts or behavior. With most of these, as with homosexual offenses, it is difficult to see what harm is done to the state, to society at large, or to other individuals—provided the acts are committed voluntarily and privately by adults. Indeed the use in privacy of animals for sexual release—a practice common enough in many U.S. rural areas to be the subject of many bawdy songs and stories—differs little in essence from solitary masturbation.

A final quartet of sex crimes, all of them centered around marriage, are bigamy, incest, seduction, and miscegenation. Bigamy must of course be forbidden in a monogamous nation. Yet the present tangle of conflicting divorce laws and requirements—coupled with the ease and popularity of peripatetic divorce—may make many a man an unwitting bigamist. Further, innocent divorce-based bigamy is almost never prosecuted except at the insistence of a supposed ex-wife out for money (to buy her off) or revenge. What is needed here is not a change in the bigamy laws but a reform of the confusion of divorce laws.

Despite the fact that Cleopatra married two of her brothers (no bigamist, she married them consecutively), incest has been taboo in most societies down through the ages and is so in the U.S. today, although different states define the crime slightly differently; first cousins living in Iowa would have to move across the state line to Minnesota to be married. Not only marriage but extramarital intercourse by close relatives is heavily punished in many states. Where the banning of such unions is based on blood relationship, laws against incest make genetic sense (although inbreeding of animals is often favored) ; but where, as in several states, incest is stretched to cover in-laws and step-children, it betrays a religious root which is largely outdated today.

Largely outdated too in the light of current sex mores, but still on most statute books, is the old crime of seduction —or persuading a girl or woman to have intercourse by a promise of marriage. Suffice it to note here that the lady must be virgin at the time of seduction, that it must be the promise, nothing else, that leads her to comply, and that the man must make the promise with deliberate intent to deceive—all rather difficult points to prove when the villain later backs away from the altar.

As for miscegenation, prohibited in very few places outside the U.S. and by barely over half of our states, the laws making it criminal are likely on their way out, courtesy of the judiciary. The California Supreme Court has declared unconstitutional that state's legal bar on interracial marriage. And only this winter, the U.S. Supreme Court vetoed a Florida ban on interracial extra-marital intercourse, while at least hinting that, when a proper case came before it, it might throw out a typical anti-miscegenation-in-marriage statute (and thus, by inference, all such statutes) as well.

Yet the task of bringing most of our sex laws up to date with our liberalized sex beliefs and sex behavior—of narrowing if not closing the hypocritical chasm between what we purport to forbid and what we *do*—is primarily and properly the job of legislators, not judges. This is what the American Law Institute's model code recognizes— and urges on the states. Not that these lawyers, backed by psychiatrists and other professional groups, are advocating an officially authorized loosening of sexual morals; they would simply have our outmoded sex-crime laws reformed —or in some instances, repealed—instead of regularly broken and ignored. And where legitimate private, as opposed to public, interests are still at stake, the law would still protect them; thus, adultery would remain a ground for divorce but not a crime.

It is a cliché that we cannot legislate morality. Even less can we legislate effectively against conduct which a large part of the community has come to accept as not immoral.

May/June 1965

Abortion Laws
And Their Victims

ALICE S. ROSSI

Millions of Americans have been personally involved in illegal abortions—the women who undergo the operations, their sex partners, and the close confidantes who share the burdens of their experiences, in most cases illegal ones. Despite this widespread personal experience, there has too long been a conspiracy of silence on the subject of abortion.

There are signs that public discussion is increasing—mass media articles, network television programs, popular movies such as "Blue Denim" and "Love with the Proper Stranger," proposals for law reform by various legal and medical bodies. But the focus of public attention is on the most dramatic, though least frequent, situations leading to the desire for abortion—conception through rape or incest, and threats to pregnancies from disease or drugs. Too little attention is paid to the overwhelming number of women who seek abortions, legal or illegal, because they do not want to give birth to an unwelcome or unexpected child.

Also, it is important to note, public discussion comes mainly from professional experts such as gynecologists, obstetricians, public health officials, and specialists in law, demography, family planning, and psychiatry. With rare exception too little is heard from the women directly concerned—those who have undergone the abortion.

Well-publicized abortion cases (such as that of Mrs. Sherry Finkbine who was eventually aborted of a deformed fetus in Europe) involve exposure to German measles during the first trimester of pregnancy or the use of thalidomide early in pregnancy, with its associated high probability of defect in the fetus. But few women who seek abortions have been exposed to German measles or taken thalidomide and hence fear a deformed fetus; few have serious heart or liver conditions that constitute a threat to their life if they carried the pregnancy to term; fewer still have been raped by a stranger or by their own father.

The majority of the women who seek abortions do so because they find themselves with unwelcome or unwanted pregnancies; abortion is a last-resort birth control measure when preventive techniques have failed or have not been used.

It is the situation *of not wanting a child* that covers the main rather than the exceptional abortion situation. But this fact is seldom faced. I believe many people are unwilling to confront this fact because it goes counter to the expectation that women are nurturant, loving creatures who welcome every new possibility of adding a member of the human race. To come to grips with the central motivation that drives women to abortion, *that they do not want the child*. requires admitting that the traditional expectation is a gross oversimplification of the nature of women and the complex of values which determine their highly individuated response to the prospects of maternity.

When a woman is anxious to conceive a child, there is nothing to match the joy that attends a confirmation that she is pregnant, except the actual birth of the baby. If we take 30 years as the fertility span of a woman, there are approximately 360 "chances" that she may become pregnant. If she wants and has three children, there will be some 325 months, or about 90 percent of her potentially fertile menstrual months, in which she does not have joyous anticipation of a pregnancy, but rather an undercurrent of feelings ranging from vague unease to considerable fear that she may be pregnant. These feelings are not completely allayed by cognitive confidence in her contraceptive technique. This is true even for women whose contraceptive practices are highly efficacious; for women who use no contraception, the apprehension is understandably more acute. Thus, one would think there would be less resistance to the idea that many women have a dread of pregnancy and, when they find themselves with an unwanted one, may seek an abortion.

Are America's laws on the subject of abortion in line with the thinking of its citizens? Before we examine the varying legal patterns—and both the campaign for reform and its opponents—let's look at the way the people view the matter.

Until very recently, there were no organized groups in the United States supporting abortion reform to match the very vigorous opposition to such reform. So legislators had no way of knowing whether the public would greet a revision in the law negatively or with a response of "it's about time." Fortunately, there are now indicators available.

A representative sample of 1,484 adult Americans were asked their views on the conditions under which it should be possible for a woman to obtain a legal abortion, in a survey conducted by the National Opinion Research Center in December 1965. These adults were asked the following question:

"Please tell me whether or not you think it should be possible for a pregnant woman to obtain a legal abortion . . ."

They were presented with six varying circumstances, ranging from impairment of the mother's health, to that of a married woman who did not want any more children. The survey results show the majority of the American population support the view that women should be able to obtain a legal abortion under the following circumstances:

■ 71 percent if the woman's own health is seriously endangered by the pregnancy.

■ 56 percent if she became pregnant as a result of rape.

■ 55 percent if there is a strong chance of serious defect in the baby.

When Catholics were compared to Protestant respondents, there was very little religious group difference. Although official Catholic doctrine makes no allowance for abortions in the event of high probability of deformity in the fetus or for pregnancies following sexual assault, close to a majority of Catholic men and women were in favor of legal abortion to cover such situations. Thus, there was no tendency to take an overall doctrinal stand against abortion among Catholics; instead, the range of support they gave varied by situation in precisely the same way that it did among Protestant or Jewish respondents.

Furthermore, the slight tendency for Protestants to be more liberal than Catholics was found to be largely a reflection of differential church attendance, not religious affiliation solely. Frequent church attenders are less likely to take a liberal stand on abortion than those who attend church less frequently *among both groups;* only because Catholics show generally higher church attendance (74 percent) than Protestants do (51 percent) was there any difference in liberal stand on abortion. The data further suggested that education has a "liberalizing" effect on the attitudes of Protestants but not of Catholics—there were no differences in attitudes among poorly educated Protestants and Catholics, but an increasing contrast as educational attainment increased.

Legislators will continue to be exposed to pressure against liberalization of the abortion laws from spokesmen of various religious faiths, but there is a clear support among the electorate from the major religious groups for revision of the existent statutes to cover not merely the life, but also the health, of a pregnant woman or serious risk of deformity in the fetus.

The study also showed that attitudes toward abortion cut across both political orientation and party lines. People with a liberal political orientation who are independent of any political party affiliation, show the most liberal attitudes toward abortion (mean of 51 percent on all six items). But at the next level of liberal views on abortion are Republicans of both liberal (47 percent) and conservative (46 percent) persuasion, and liberal Democrats (42 percent). Those least sympathetic to abortion law reform are conservative Democrats (36 percent) and those who are either politically uncommitted or apolitical.

What the American public clearly does *not* support, however, are abortions in situations which all studies indicate to be the predominant circumstances for women who seek abortions. Support for legal abortions in the remaining three situations is as follows:

■ 21 percent if the family has a very low income and cannot afford any more children.

■ 18 percent if she is not married and does not want to marry the man.

■ 15 percent if she is married and wants no more children. The analysis showed no differences between Catholics and Protestants on these grounds. What mattered more was education, sex, and general attitude toward sex. Men with at least some college education, for example, are far more likely to approve legal abortions in the case of an un-married pregnant woman (33 percent) than are women who have had some college training (19 percent) or men (19 percent) and women (9 percent) who have never gone beyond elementary school.

Restrictive attitudes toward premarital sex bear a decided relationship to opposition to legal abortion for every one of the six conditions we specified. Men and women who op-pose premarital intercourse between an engaged couple are considerably less likely to approve a legal abortion than those who have a permissive or ambivalent attitude toward premarital intercourse—even where maternal health is en-dangered or the woman has been sexually assaulted. It is of interest that there are no attitude differences about abor-tion between men and women among those who hold *re-strictive* views toward premarital sex relations; but among those with *permissive* attitudes, men are much more in-clined than women to support legal abortions as birth con-trol measures.

Overall then, there is clearly majority support for abor-tion as a safeguard of maternal health or a prevention of the anguish associated with bearing a deformed child. But any suggestion of abortion as a last-resort means of birth control is firmly rejected by the majority of American adults in the NORC sample. It does not seem to matter what the circumstances are—a poor family for whom an additional child would represent an economic hardship, a single woman who does not wish to marry the man with whom she had sex relations, or a married woman who does not want any more children. The American population approves family planning by means of acceptable contraceptive techniques, but any failure of traditional birth control measures should be followed not by an abortion, but by an acceptance of the pregnancy.

The fact that the last condition—of a married woman who has the number of children she wants—has been the experience of millions of living American women, has not affected public judgment that abortion is "wrong" and should not be legally allowed. The suggestion is strong, therefore, that Americans disapprove of any legitimate institutionalization of a widespread practice if the practice runs counter to the traditional social and religious norms surrounding sex and maternity.

Let us turn now to the law. The perspective of a sociologist and a woman may, it is hoped, contribute to keeping the complex legal and medical considerations from deflecting our attention from the central problem at stake—what society should do for a woman facing an unwanted pregnancy.

State laws vary in the language used and whether the focus is on the mother alone or the mother and the child. In 32 states abortions are unlawful unless they are necessary to "save" or "preserve" the life of the mother. In nine states the preservation of life covers the mother or her child. In only five states and the District of Columbia does the letter of the law go beyond the restriction to saving a life; in Colorado and New Mexico abortions are permitted to preserve the mother's life or prevent "serious bodily injury"; in Alabama, Oregon, and the District of Columbia, the law exempts abortions designed to preserve the life or "health" of the mother. Only in Maryland is the legal phrasing more general: the state law exempts abortions which would "secure the safety of the mother."

These statutes come under the criminal code. The goal of abortion reform groups has been concentrated on seeking a change in this penal code. Revision proposals are most frequently based on the Model Penal Code recommended by the American Law Institute in 1959. The clauses relevant to abortion extend exemption from criminal prosecution to cases in which the continuance of the pregnancy involves "substantial risk that mother or child will suffer grave and irremediable impairment of physical or mental health" or where the pregnancy "resulted from forcible rape." Thus, if there is a high probability of defect in the fetus or serious physical or psychological impairment of the mother should she carry the fetus to term, and if the presence of these circumstances is certified by at least two physicians, then a legal abortion will be possible under this revised code, and the doctors involved have a justifiable affirmative defense.

It is this revised penal code clause which has received rather widespread endorsement. Variations of it have been reviewed and hearings held in the legislatures of several states—Illinois, Minnesota, New Hampshire, California, and New York. In no case has reform yet succeeded. So too, the recommendation of the Committee on Human Reproduction of the AMA favoring law reform was turned down by the House of Delegates of the AMA, which referred the problem back to the Board of Trustees with a recommendation that the problem be explored "in depth with other interested groups."

Where illegal abortion is concerned, the estimated range of operations is from 250,000 to somewhat over 1,000,000 per year in the United States. We are on somewhat firmer ground in gauging the incidence of legal abortions conducted in hospital settings, particularly when they are based on statistics from municipalities in which such abortions are required to be justified and recorded. The most recent estimate for the United States is somewhere between 8,000 and 10,000.

Yet, to many people opposed to law reform this is not a "significant" problem because there is no agreement on exactly how extensive the incidence of illegal abortion is. Further, many persons refuse to believe even the lower limit of the estimated range, on the grounds that they personally know of no woman who has had an illegal abortion.

Also, they say, there is no need to change the law because abortion is declining, as contraceptive practices become more widespread and more effective.

Is the incidence rate a proper basis for deciding whether this is a major social problem or not? Medical researchers do not avoid attempts to find a cure for a rare disease because the chances are it will cripple or kill only 10,000 people a year. We do not consider unemployment a minor social problem because more than 90 percent of the labor force is employed. We do not rest content with educational attainment of American youth because the majority now complete a high school education.

The same reasoning should apply to the abortion problem. Those who argue with the incidence estimates, or resist change in our abortion laws on the grounds that it is not an extensive social problem, are either deluding us or themselves as to what is really at the heart of their disclaimers: they do not wish to see any liberalization of abortion laws because they are opposed to abortion per se; or they have little or no empathy for the women who want to obtain one; or they consciously or unconsciously believe the psychologically punishing and medically and legally risky experience of securing an illegal abortion is deserved —it is a *punishment* for becoming pregnant if you are poor or unmarried or already have a large family.

There is enormous variation from hospital to hospital, city to city, one physician to another in the ratio of therapeutic abortions to deliveries. One doctor may perform one abortion to every four or five deliveries, while another performs one abortion to every 2,000 deliveries. A private hospital with financially well-off patients, may perform one legal abortion in every 36 deliveries, while another hospital, one which treats clinic patients, has a record of no legal abortions in 24,417 deliveries.

The grounds justifying legal therapeutic abortions have changed over the years. Psychological justification has increased as strictly medical considerations of physical health have declined. Doctors have shown a gradual broadening of their conception of "health" to include many non-physical factors in the woman's condition, a reflection of the slow penetration of psychoanalytic theory into medical training and medical thinking. The decline in abortions for medical reasons is also a reflection of medical progress: as tuberculosis declined in the population at large, so it declined as justification for legal abortions. As knowledge is acquired about the effect of radiation, rubella, or thalidomide upon the probability of defect in the fetus, new grounds for legal abortion enter the picture.

Following the model of the Scandinavian countries, there has been a marked trend in the United States since the 1950's toward the establishment of hospital abortion boards to review potential cases of abortion. Studies have shown that hospitals following this committee device have lower therapeutic abortion rates than hospitals without such committees; the establishment of the committees can be interpreted as a self-protecting response on the part of the medical profession against the trend toward an increasing number of legal abortions for psychological reasons.

The effect of liberalization of abortion laws upon subsequent patterns of live births and abortion rates can be gleaned by analysis of data from other countries. One pattern is clear: the birth rate declines more rapidly following such abortion liberalization than by any comparable measure such as contraceptive campaigns. This is nowhere more dramatically shown than in Japan since the passage of the Eugenic Protection Law in 1948. This act comes closer to abortion-on-demand than any abortion legislation anywhere in the world. The success of this policy in halting the skyrocketing population increase in Japan can be seen by comparing the rate of live births and of legal abortions in the year following the passage of the act, 1949, and comparable rates for 1962: the rate of live births per 1,000 population declined from 33.2 in 1949 to 17.0 in 1962, while the rate of legal abortions per 1,000 population increased from 3.0 to 10.4. This rapid increase in abortions during the 1950's was due mainly to older women aborting pregnancies after they already had a number of children.

Much the same story applies to countries in Eastern Europe. In Hungary, for example, which introduced interruption of pregnancy "on-request" in 1956, the number of legal abortions increased rapidly; by 1961 abortions exceeded the number of live births by more than one-fifth. The fact that the birth rate declined in East European countries which have liberalized abortion laws, but did *not* decline in the two countries which did not legalize abortion

(Albania and East Germany) is strong evidence that the legalization of abortion depressed the birth rate.

It may be, incidentally, that the most dramatic birth rate reduction, in countries whose population is growing at alarming rates, would result from a two-part program: liberalization of abortion laws which women will respond to (pregnancy being primarily "women's concern"), and contraceptive campaigns aimed at the men (sex being "men's concern").

What is known about the pattern of *illegal abortion* cases is necessarily on less confident grounds:

■ **Roughly** one in five of the women in the Kinsey study who were ever married reported induced abortions. While this sample is not completely representative of the American population, somewhat greater confidence can be placed in the Kinsey picture of subgroup variations in the proportion reporting induced abortions. They found that induced abortions increase with the number of pregnancies terminated in marriage, testimony to the fact that women resort to abortion for pregnancies which occur after they have reached the family size they desire. The relationship shown by age and education is similarly interesting for the social pattern it suggests: among poorly educated women, the highest rate of induced abortion is among the older women; among well-educated women, the highest rate is among the younger women. What this suggests is that poorly educated women who become pregnant, either have illegitimate children (particularly if they are Negro), or marry and have the first child within wedlock, and abort their later pregnancies. Well-educated women abort their premarital pregnancies, marry later and use more reliable contraceptive techniques with more cooperative husbands to control their family size.

■ The abortion rate, like the fertility rate, is responsive

to the economic cycle in the society. By comparing the rate of reported induced abortions with the age when they were performed, Paul Gebhard shows that abortions were probably greater during the depression and declined in the 1940's and 1950's.

The official Catholic position on abortion has held simply that nothing may be done which would involve any direct killing of the fetus. The only exception is the application of the Catholic rule of "double effect" or "indirect killing." Catholic obstetricians may remove an ectopic pregnancy or a cancerous pregnant uterus because these operations have the primary purpose of saving the life of the mother, not the killing of the fetus, which is secondary.

Whatever the position of the church, the actual behavior of Catholics is quite another matter. Countries with predominantly Roman Catholic populations actually show high abortion rates, as they do of illegitimacy. In a recent survey of Roman Catholic Chile, for example, 27 percent of the women reported they had had induced abortions. In Roman Catholic France, the annual number of abortions equals the annual number of live births.

A religious group is free to characterize abortion as a sin if it sees fit to do so and to punish its members for this by some appropriate ecclesiastical censure if it wishes. The rest of the society should, however, enjoy the right to control their own reproductive lives in accordance with their conception of morality and human dignity.

Apart from the fine points of theology and ethical consideration, there is a quality of sentimentality about the defense of the right of the fetus to be born that strikes at least this feminine ear as alien to the ways and the feelings of women one has known or studied. I have never heard a woman wax sentimental about 300 or so ova which are never fertilized, nor have I heard remorse expressed for a two-month-old fetus that is spontaneously aborted. It is not the loss of a particular fetus a woman grieves over, but the loss of her potential maternity and potential baby. In a similar way, despite all claims to the contrary, there is no evidence that women who have had induced abortions are typically stricken with guilt and remorse as an aftermath. The few cases of women who do feel such regret must be weighed against the human price in bitterness, economic hardship, and psychological stress that is paid by the woman, her family, and the unwanted child if she does *not* obtain an abortion.

It would appear to be a matter of time and the continued and extended efforts of men and women who work for abortion reform, until American law will undergo some degree of liberalization. It is still an open question, however, how widespread the trend will be in various states to remove abortion from coverage by the criminal law (no other medical procedure is regulated by criminal law) and to place it under either civil statutes bearing on the licensing of physicians, or, more positively, statutes bearing on the regulation of hospitals. Either of these latter two changes would clearly and firmly shift responsibility to the medical profession.

But if we rest content with goals limited to the penal code revision that is most likely to be passed, we shall scarcely have helped many women in the United States. Nor will such passage of a revised code be followed by any significant increase in legal abortions and decrease in illegal abortions, since the law will not cover most of the women who now have abortions illegally. Married women who do not want to have a third or fourth child (or an unmarried woman who does not want to marry the man by whom she has conceived, or who does not want to marry her) will still be faced with a cruel choice between deceitful lying in order to get a legal abortion, or being honest about her motivation and seeking an illegal one.

Let us take, as an example, the plight of an unmarried woman who becomes pregnant. What alternatives does our society offer her, and what is the consequence for the woman and for the society?

■ *Marry the man by whom she conceived.* The price?— a high-risk marriage. There is no period for the mutual exploration of each other and adjustment to marriage itself, but a double task of adjusting to pregnancy and anticipated maternity while also adjusting to spouse, sex, and obligations of home maintenance. The outcome—a high probability of divorce and separation, a couple cheated of the joy and adventure and independence of the pre-parenthood stage of marriage, more children reared in fatherless homes, and strained relations between the woman and her parents, who are so often firmly insistent on the daughter's marriage as the solution to her pregnancy out of wedlock.

■ *Go through with the pregnancy and put the child up for adoption.* There are few writers in the literature on abortion who have stressed what many women in this situation feel deeply—the cruelty and sadism that is involved when her doctor, parents, minister, lawyer, or social worker suggest that she carry the child to term and then hand it over, never to see it again, to someone else to raise. It is a heartless recommendation, and psychiatrists inform us it creates far more difficult and extensive therapeutic problems than with patients who have an abortion early in pregnancy.

■ *Have the child illegitimately and rear it herself.* The price? Ask those engaged currently in trying to break the vicious cycle of poverty in the lower working class of our large cities: women with double responsibility as breadwinner and mother working at jobs for which they do not receive equal pay for equal work; encounters with men who do not want to assume responsibility for another man's child; children who often suffer from neglect to outright maternal rejection.

■ *Have an abortion*—if she has the good fortune to contact a physician courageous enough to recommend her for a legal abortion, or refer her to another physician for an illegal abortion.

To withhold the possibility of a safe and socially acceptable abortion for unmarried women is to start the chain of illegitimacy and despair that will continue to keep poverty, crime, and poor mental health high on the list of pressing social problems in the United States. Finally, it is expecting entirely too much of human frailty and the complex motivations underlying human sexual behavior to think abortions will no longer be necessary when contraceptive techniques are perfected and universally used. One has only to observe carefully the adaptive role the woman plays in sex in Mirra Komarovsky's *Blue Collar Marriage* or Lee Rainwater's *Workingman's Wife* and *And the Poor Get Children* to understand some of the limitations upon the consistent use of contraceptives by large numbers of American women. Furthermore, not all women can take the pill, nor be fitted with a ring, and pregnancies even occur in both types of birth control.

Social approval is extended to the woman who plans her family size and child spacing well by using the best contraceptive technique available and suitable for her, but if these measures fail, the only alternative is acceptance of pregnancy she does not want, or the unsafe and traumatic experience of an illegal abortion. Any woman, whether married or not, should be able to secure a safe abortion, upon her own request, at a reasonable fee, in a licensed hospital by a licensed and competent physician.

September 1966

Sexual Assaults
in the
Philadelphia Prison System

ALAN J. DAVIS

In the summer of 1968, Joseph F. Mitchell, a slightly-built 19-year-old, was brought to trial before Alexander F. Barbieri, judge of the Court of Common Pleas No. 8 in Philadelphia County. Mitchell's lawyer, Joseph E. Alessandroni, told Judge Barbieri that his client, while being transported in a sheriff's van, had been repeatedly raped by a gang of criminals. A few weeks later, Alessandroni informed the judge that George Di-Angelo, a slender 21-year-old whom Barbieri had committed to the Philadelphia Detention Center merely for pre-sentence evaluation, had been sexually assaulted within minutes of his admission.

Judge Barbieri thereupon appointed me, then Chief Assistant District Attorney of Philadelphia, to investigate these allegations. Police Commissioner Frank L. Rizzo started a parallel investigation; then these two investigations were merged.

In the Philadelphia prison system there are three facilities: the Detention Center, Holmesburg Prison, and the House of Correction. The period we chose to study was from June 1966 to July 31, 1968—a little over two years. Out of the 60,000 inmates who passed through the prison system in those 26 months, we interviewed 3,304—virtually all of them inmates during the period of our investigation. We also interviewed 561 out of the 570 custodial employees. We took 130 written statements from those who had given us important information, and gave polygraph ("lie-detector") examinations to 45 of them. We asked 26 employees to take polygraph tests: 25 refused, and the one employee who took the test "passed." We asked 48 inmates: seven refused, and of the 41 remaining, 10 failed the test and 31 passed. (We ignored the statements of those prisoners and employees who either would not take the test or who failed it.) In addition, we interviewed several people whom we believed had special information, and we reviewed all of the reports dealing with homosexuality issued by the prison system since June 1966. Finally, we made a number of detailed personal inspections of the prison facilities and of the sheriff's vans.

In brief, we found that sexual assaults in the Philadelphia prison system are epidemic. As Superintendent Hendrick and three of the wardens admitted, virtually every slightly-built young man committed by the courts is sexually approached within a day or two after his admission to prison. Many of these young men are repeatedly raped by gangs of inmates. Others, because of the threat of gang rape, seek protection by entering into a homosexual relationship with an individual tormentor. Only the tougher and more hardened young men, and those few so obviously frail that they are immediately locked up for their own protection, escape homosexual rape.

After a young man has been raped, he is marked as a sexual victim for the duration of his confinement. This mark follows him from institution to institution. Many of these young men return to their communities ashamed, and full of hatred.

This, then, is the sexual system that exists in the Philadelphia prisons. It is a system that imposes a punishment that is not, and could not be, included in the sentence of the court. Indeed, it is a system under which the least hardened criminals, and many men later found to be innocent, suffer the most.

A few typical examples of such sexual assaults may convey the enormity of the problem. In an early draft of our report, an attempt was made to couch this illustrative material in sociological, medical, and legal terminology less offensive than the raw, ugly language used by the witness and victims. This approach was abandoned. The incidents are raw and ugly. Any attempt to prettify them would be hypocrisy.

A witness describes the ordeal of *William McNichol*. 24 years old and mentally disturbed:

"That was June 11th, I was assigned to E Dorm. Right after the light went out I saw this colored male, Cheyenne—I think his last name is Boone. He went over and was talking to this kid and slapped him in the face with a belt. He was saying come on back with us and the kid kept saying I don't want to. After being slapped with the belt he walked back with Cheyenne and another colored fellow named Horse. They were walking him back into E Dorm. They were telling him to put his hand down and stop crying so the guard will not know what is going on. I looked up a couple of times. They had the kid on the floor. About 12 fellows took turns with him. This went on for about two hours.

"After this he came back to his bed and he was crying and he stated that 'They all took turns on me.' He laid there for about 20 minutes and Cheyenne came over to the kid's bed and pulled his pants down and got on top of him and raped him again. When he got done Horse did it again and then about four or five others got on him. While one of the guys was on him, raping him, Horse came over and said, 'Open your mouth and suck on this and don't bite it.' He then put his penis in his mouth and made him suck on it. The kid was hollering that he was gagging and Horse stated, 'you better not bite it or I will kick your teeth out.'

"While they had this kid they also had a kid named William in another section in E Dorm. He had his pants off and he was bent over and they were taking turns on him. This was Horse, Cheyenne, and about seven other colored fellows. Two of the seven were brothers.

"Horse came back and stated, 'Boy, I got two virgins in one night. Maybe I should make it three.' At this time he was standing over me. I stated, 'What are you looking at?' and he said 'We'll save him for tomorrow night.' "

Julius Brown, 18 years old:

"Brown stated that he has been in Holmesburg since March 29, 1968, and that about a week and a half ago, on Thursday, he was in I block; his cell was number 926. On this date, in the morning after breakfast, James Williams called him into his cell; he went into William's cell. Donald Reese was in there also. Further that he had owed Williams four cartons of cigarettes.

Williams said to him that he would have to give the cigarettes back right now or he would have to give them something else. He [Brown] then started to walk out of the cell and Williams pushed him down. Williams picked up the window pole, Reese picked up a bench and stood blocking the door. Reese told him that if he goes to the guard they are going to get him anyway; there were other men outside the cell.

"Further that he walked out of the cell, they were all around him and walked to cell 971, and they pushed him inside. He went over and sat on the toilet seat. Twin [Roger Jones] came into the cell, they made him lay down on the floor, and Twin pulled his [Brown's] pants down and made him lay face down. Twin pushed his [Brown's] legs apart and Twin put his penis into his [Brown's] rectum. He was on him until he discharged. When he got through, Brown saw that he was bleeding from the rectum. Then Twin, Williams, Reese, and McDuffy told him that if he went to the guard their boys would get him to D block, and he was scared then to tell the guard. Further that he did cry out when Twin did this to him, but the guard wouldn't be able to hear him because the block is long.

"Brown went on to say that the next day after chow [breakfast] James Williams, McDuffy, Ike (Isaiah Franklin), and Leftenant got him in cell 972 [Roger Jones's cell]. They told him that everything is cool now as long as he doesn't tell. Further that he had never been in jail before and he was too scared to tell anybody. Then four of them did it to him—they put their penises into his rectum, James first, Ike second, Leftenant third, McDuffy fourth. Twin did not bother him that time. That after they did this he was bleeding and got sick.

"That night, Roach [Thomas Roach] came into his cell and changed with his partner. Roach told him that he would have to do it. When the guard came to check the cells, Roach turned over so he wouldn't be recognized. After the guard counted and left, Roach got on top of him, put his penis into his [Brown's] rectum, and discharged."

Charles Williams, 19 years old:
"On Tuesday morning, the first week of June at about 9:30 A.M., I was in my cell 412 on D block and I had started to clean up. A tall, heavy-set fella came into the cell and asked for a mirror and shaving brush and a comb, and that my cell partner said he could borrow.

"He then said that he heard something about me concerning homosexual acts. I told him what he had heard was not true. He then started to threaten me and if I didn't submit to him. Then I hit him with my fist in his face before he could hit me. Then about three more men came into the cell, and they started to beat me up, too. I fought back the best I could and then I fell on the floor and I got kicked in the ribs. Three guys were holding me while the other one tore my pants off; I continued to fight until one of the guys knocked me out. One of the guys was holding me on the floor and had my arm pinned to the floor. And about seven or eight guys came into the cell and they took turns sticking their penis up my ass. When they finished they left my cell, and I was still laying on the floor."

Clarence Garlick, 26 years old:
"Back in April this year, about 10:30 A.M. I was in my cell 455 on block D when Joe Lovett came into my cell. I was laying on my bed. When he came in I jumped up. He told me to get greased up. I told him

I wasn't going to do nothing. He told me, 'You're going to do something.' He started punching me. I had backed up into a corner of the cell. He seen some mineral-oil grease I had on the table and he reached over and handed it to me saying, 'Put this on.' I put some on and layed down on the bed. He took out his penis and got on top of me. After he did what he wanted to do he got up and got some toilet paper and wiped himself off and went out of the cell."

"This is the second incident. He came to me on July 18, 1968, in the morning about 10 o'clock. I was standing up in the doorway of my cell, 455. He told me to 'Get it fixed.' I told him I wasn't going to do nothing, that today was my birthday. He walked on away."

"The next day, on the 19th, he came to me again. I was in my cell, this was about the same time. He stated, 'Today isn't your birthday, you're going to do something.' I told him I wasn't going to do anything. He started punching me again. I told him I was going to call the guard. He stated, 'Go ahead and call, you'll only call him one time and I'll knock you out.' He got the grease from off the table and handed it to me, told me to put some on, which I did. I laid down on the bed, he took out his penis and got on top. A friend he walks with, Kincaid, was standing out by the door, he was laughing. Joe got up after he got through, got toilet paper and wiped himself off. He then walked out of the cell."

During the 26-month period, we found, there had been 156 sexual assaults that could be documented and substantiated—through institutional records, polygraph examinations, or other corroboration. Seven of the assaults took place in the sheriff's vans, 149 in the prisons. Of the sexual assaults, 82 consisted of buggery; 19 of fellatio; and 55 of attempts and coercive solicitations to commit sexual acts. There were assaults on at least 97 different victims by at least 176 different aggressors. With unidentified victims and aggressors, there were 109 different victims and 276 different aggressors.

For various reasons, these figures represent only the top of the iceberg.

■ Our investigators, as mentioned, interviewed only a twentieth of the inmates who passed through the prison system. We discovered 94 assaults—excluding those reported in institutional records. This suggests that if all 60,000 inmates had been interviewed, 20 times 94—or 1880—additional assaults would have come to light.

■ Almost all of the victims still in prison were so terrified of retaliation by other prisoners that they were very reluctant to cooperate with us.

■ Many guards discouraged complaints by indicating that they did not want to be bothered. One victim screamed for over an hour while he was being gang-raped in his cell; the block guard ignored the screams and laughed at the victim when the rape was over. The inmates who reported this passed a polygraph examination. The guard who had been named refused to take the test.

Then too, some guards put pressure on victims not to complain—such complaints, after all, would indicate that the guards were failing in their duty. We found many cases where victims, after filing complaints, had "voluntarily" refused to prosecute, and a number of them told us that guards urged them to rely on prison discipline rather than to bring the facts out into the open. Very often, these guards asked the victim if he wanted his parents and friends to find out about his humiliation.

■ Without prompting from the prison guards, many victims and their families wanted to avoid the shame and dishonor they believed would follow such a complaint.

■ Inmates have little faith in the ability of a guard to protect them from retaliation should they complain. Their fears are justified by the lack of supervision by guards, and the inadequate facilities to provide security for complainants.

■ Inmates who complain are themselves punished by the prison system. It is usual procedure to place a victim of a sexual assault on "lock-in feed-in," obstensibly for his own protection. This means that after a complaint is made, and especially if it is pressed, the complainant is locked in his cell all day, fed in his cell, and not permitted recreation, television, or exercise until it is determined that he is safe from retaliation. Many victims consider this "solitary confinement" worse than a homosexual relationship with one aggressor.

■ Sometimes very little comes of a complaint. Some compaints are just not acted upon; action, when taken, usually consists of putting the aggressor in the "hole" for 30 days or less. Meanwhile, the victim also is usually locked in, and looks forward—when released—to terror from the aggressor's friends, and from the aggressor himself when he is let out of the "hole." Finally,

■ Many of the victims themselves distrust and are hostile to constituted authority, and could not bring themselves to cooperate by filing a complaint.

Taking all of these facts into consideration, we conservatively estimate that the true number of assaults in the 26-month period was about 2000. Indeed, one guard put the number at 250 a year in the Detention Center alone.

Of the estimated 2000 assaults that occurred, 156 of which were documented, the inmates reported only 96 to prison authorities. Of this 96, only 64 were mentioned in the prison records. Of these 64, only 40 resulted in internal discipline against the aggressors; and only 26 incidents were reported to the police for prosecution.

Now, in our study of sexual assaults we excluded any that were cases of truly "consensual" homosexuality. Nonetheless, it was hard to separate consensual homosexuality from rape, since many continuing and isolated homosexual liaisons originated from a gang rape, or from the ever-present threat of gang rape. Similarly, many individual homosexual acts were possible only because of the fear-charged atmosphere. Thus, a threat of rape, expressed or implied, would prompt an already fearful young man to submit. Prison officials are too quick to label such activities "consensual."

At the opposite end of the spectrum from innocent victims of homosexual rape are the male prostitutes. These homosexuals—known as "sissys," "freaks," or "girls"—were supposed to be segregated from the general prison population, yet they were readily available. We learned of repeated instances where homosexual "security" cells were left unguarded by a staff that was too small or too indifferent, or who turned their backs so that certain favored inmates could have sexual relations.

Many of these male prostitutes were created not only by force and the threat of force, but by bribery. The fact is that a person with economic advantage in prison often uses it to gain sexual advantage. Typically, an experienced inmate will give cigarettes, candy, sedatives, stainless-steel blades, or extra food pilfered from the kitchen to an inexperienced inmate, and after a few days the veteran will demand sexual repayment. It is also typical for a veteran to entice a young man into gambling, have him roll up large debts, and then tell the youth to "pay or fuck." An initial sexual act stamps the victim as a "punk boy," and he is pressed into prostitution for the remainder of his imprisonment.

Despite the important role that economic advantage plays in the creation of homosexuality, it is virtually impossible to obliterate economic distinctions between inmates. Even a small accumulation of money or luxuries gives an inmate substantial economic advantage: In the prison economy, a shopworker earns 15 to 25 cents a day; half of the inmates have no prison jobs at all, and most inmates get little or no material help from friends or relatives outside the prison.

It is the duty of prison officials to reduce the economic power that any inmate might exercise over another inmate. Yet we discovered one area in which Philadelphia prison officials, either through neglect or indifference, disregarded this duty. As a result, at least one inmate became so powerful economically that he was able to choose, as cellmates, a series of young men he found attractive, and then use bribery to sexually subvert each one.

The University of Pennsylvania and a private concern operate a large laboratory on H block of Holmesburg Prison, where they test inmates' reactions to new medicines and to experimental commercial products like soaps, shaving creams, suntan lotions, and toilet tissue. The prisoners are excellent "human guinea pigs" (1) because they live under controlled conditions, and

(2) because they will submit to tests for a fraction of the fee that a free individual would demand. Prison officials—because there is very little other activity for the prisoners, and because the laboratory pays 20 percent of the inmates' wages to the prison system—have allowed the project to expand to the extent that it constitutes a separate government within the prison system.

All the inmates at Holmesburg wanted to "get on the tests" because, by prison standards, they can earn a fortune. Just by wearing a chemical patch on his back, for example, a prisoner can earn $10 to $15 a week. By participating in some tests that last longer, a prisoner—for doing almost nothing—will receive over $100. Altogether, the Holmesburg inmates earn more than $250,000 a year from the project. A few prisoners end up with bodies crazyquilted with motley scars and skin patches, but to these men, in the context of a prison economy, it seems well worth it.

To save money another way, the operators of the project also use inmates as laboratory assistants. An experienced assistant, working an eight-hour day, will get $100 a month—in the prison economy, the equivalent of a millionaire's income. Even a few prison guards are employed in the project, after their regular hours, and they work side by side with the prisoners.

Generally, the "U. of P." project has had a disastrous effect upon the operations of Holmesburg Prison; it is one of the reasons why morale of the employees is at the lowest in that institution. The disproportionate wealth and power in the hands of a few inmates leads to favoritism, bribery and jealousy among the guards, resulting in disrespect for supervisory authority and prison regulations. What is more, the project contributed to homosexuality in the prison.

Stanley Randall, a 38-year-old con man serving a four- to eleven-year sentence, was employed in laboratory cell 806, H block, as an assistant. Although prison and laboratory officials at first denied it, Randall had the power to decide which inmates would serve as subjects on various tests. Since the 806 cell disbursed $10,000 to $20,000 a year, Randall's power was considerable.

Randall's special taste was newly admitted young inmates. Through his influence with the guard staff he had his pick of these young men assigned to him as cellmates—and for as long as he wished. When his victims moved in, Randall solicited them to engage in sexual acts in return for his giving them a steady stream of luxuries and for "getting them on the tests." At least half a dozen of these inmates submitted, and went on to profit handsomely from the University of Pennsylvania project.

Although top prison officials assured us that no inmate was permitted to earn more than $1200 a year, and that $400 was unusually high, in six months Randall's present cellmate had earned over $800. The record was held by a prior cellmate of Randall's, who had earned $1740 in just 11 months. When we asked university project managers about these high incomes, they told us they had never heard of any $1200-a-year-limit. The prison's accounting office had apparently never heard of this $1200-a-year limit either, because that office had credited these high amounts to the accounts of Randall's cellmates.

How had Randall managed to get his choice of cellmates? One guard told us that H-block guards had been instructed by "higher ups" not to interfere in the affairs of inmates working for the U. of P. Another guard reported he had received such instructions, and said they had come from the guard lieutenant. The lieutenant denied this, and agreed to take a lie-detector test. Later he reversed his position and refused. Randall admitted he had often given cigars to this lieutenant.

Other inmates besides Randall exploited their powerful positions. One inmate worker, for example, forged test results and fee vouchers, and got fees for inmates who had not actually been test subjects. It also seems that at least a few guards were also corrupted.

As a result of our investigation, prison officials have relieved the powerful inmate workers of their positions with the U. of P. project. They are also considering phasing out the project entirely.

How did sexual aggressors in the prisons differ from their victims? On the average, aggressors tended to be older, heavier, taller, and more serious offenders. Data on hundreds of victims and aggressors yielded the following comparisons:

	Victims	Aggressors
Average Age	20.75	23.67
Average Height	5'8¼"	5'9"
Average Weight	140.9	157.2

Both victims and aggressors tended to be younger than the average inmate, as comparison with the following table shows:

Average Age of Prisoners (July 31, 1968)	
Detention Center	27.9
Holmesburg	29.3
House of Correction	28.9
All Prisons	28.8

Yet although aggressors on the average are older and larger than victims, these differences are rather slight. In many cases, there may be no differences, and in others they are reversed. Still, after having observed hundreds of victims and aggressors we believe that there are other, more subjective, physical criteria which can be used to differentiate between aggressors and victims:

■ Victims tend to look young for their age.

■ Victims tend to look less athletic, and less physically coordinated.

■ Victims tend to be better-looking.

A comparison of 164 aggressors and 103 victims showed that 68 percent of the former and only 38 percent of the latter had been charged with serious felonies. Among aggressors, violent assaultive felonies were particularly common. Thus, 14 aggressors had been charged with rape, but only three victims; six aggressors had been charged with weapons offenses, and no victims; 34 aggressors with robbery and aggravated robbery, but only eight victims; and seven aggressors with assault with intent to kill, but only one victim.

As many victims as aggressors, however, had been charged with homicide. On the other hand, many more victims than aggressors were charged with relatively less serious offenses, such as the larceny of a car, going AWOL from the armed forces, violating parole, and delinquency.

We also made a study of the 129 documented assaults in which the races of both aggressors and victims had been ascertained, and found that a disproportionate number involved Negro aggressors and white victims:

Type of Incident	Number of Incidents	Percentage
White Aggressors & White Victims	20	15%
Negro Aggressors & Negro Victims	37	29%
White Aggressors & Negro Victims	0	0%
Negro Aggressors & White Victims	72	56%
Total	129	100%

These statistics in part reflect the fact that 80 percent of the inmates are Negro—it is safer for a member of a majority group to single out for attack a member of a minority group. Then too, Negro victims seemed more reluctant than white victims to disclose assaults by Negro aggressors. But it also seems true that current racial tensions and hostilities in the outside community are aggravated in a criminal population.

Now, we are not professionally qualified to offer a scientific theory to explain the sexual aggression in the Philadelphia prison system. We have, however, reached certain conclusions that should be recorded for possible use by psychiatrists, psychologists, and social scientists. The conclusions and the analysis set forth are based upon our observations, upon pertinent literature, and upon discussions with a psychiatrist and a psychologist who are experts in forensic psychology.

■ We were struck by the fact that the typical sexual aggressor does not consider himself to be a homosexual, or even to have engaged in homosexual acts. This seems to be based upon his startlingly primitive view of sexual relationships, one that defines as male whichever partner is aggressive and as homosexual whichever partner is passive.

■ It appears that need for sexual release is not the primary motive of a sexual aggressor. After all, in a sexually segregated population, autoeroticism would seem a much easier and more "normal" method of release than homosexual rape. As recent studies have shown (Masters and Johnson, *Human Sexual Response*, 1966), autoerotic stimulation yields a measure of physical release and pleasure similar to that yielded by sexual intercourse.

■ A primary goal of the sexual aggressor, it is clear, is the conquest and degradation of his victim. We repeatedly found that aggressors used such language as "Fight or fuck," "We're going to take your manhood," "You'll have to give up some face," and "We're gonna make a girl out of you." Some of the assaults were reminiscent of the custom in some ancient societies of castrating or buggering a defeated enemy.

■ Another primary goal of many of the aggressors, it appears, is to retain membership in the groups led by militant sexual aggressors. This is particularly true of some of the participants in gang rapes. Lacking identification with such groups, as many of the aggressors know, they themselves would become victims. And finally,

■ Most of the aggressors seem to be members of a subculture that has found most nonsexual avenues of asserting their masculinity closed to them. To them, job success, raising a family, and achieving the respect of other men socially have been largely beyond reach. Only sexual and physical prowess stands between them and a feeling of emasculation. When the fact of imprisonment, and the emptiness of prison life, knock from under them whatever props to their masculinity they may have had, they became almost totally dependent for self-esteem upon an assertion of their sexual and physical potency.

In sum, sexual assaults, as opposed to consensual homosexuality, are not primarily caused by sexual deprivation. They are expressions of anger and aggression prompted by the same basic frustrations that exist in the community, and which very probably were significant factors in producing the rapes, robberies, and other violent offenses for which the bulk of the aggressors were convicted. These frustrations can be summarized as an inability to achieve masculine identification and pride through avenues other than sex. When these frustrations are intensified by imprisonment, and superimposed upon hostility between the races and a simplistic view of all sex as an act of aggression and subjugation, then the result is assaults on members of the same sex.

Assuming that this analysis is valid, then the principal psychological causes of sexual assaults in the Philadelphia prison system are deeply rooted in the community—in that millions of American men, throughout their lives, are deprived of any effective way of achieving masculine self-identification through avenues other than physical aggression and sex. They belong to a class of men who rarely have meaningful work, successful families, or opportunities for constructive emotional expression and individual creativity. Therefore, although sexual assaults within a prison system may be controlled by intensive supervision and effective programing, the pathology at the root of sexual assaults will not be eliminated until fundamental changes are made in the outside community.

December 1968

Lesbian Liaisons

DAVID A. WARD/GENE G. KASSEBAUM

How do women react to the deprivations, limitations, and degradations of prison? Almost all of what is known about adaptations prisoners make, the defenses they create, the way they strike back, compensate, or resign themselves, refers to prisons for men. Much less is known about women. It is not clear whether the needs and behavior of women in prison are substantially different than those of men or whether the effects of being imprisoned are so uniform and overriding that similarities become greater than differences.

Mrs. Iverne R. Carter, superintendent of the California Institution for Women, the largest women's prison in the world, has challenged the assumption that female prisoners require the same kind of management as do males. She has said that in her experience they act differently, have different problems, and, consequently, they need different treatment.

To examine the behavior of women in prison the authors initiated a study at the California Institution for Women in 1961. Over a two-year period data were gathered through the use of interviews, questionnaires, personal observation, and detailed analysis of official records. Support for the superintendent's statement was found:

▪ Women do not appear to have as high a level of informal community organization and solidarity as do male prisoners. They do not support "convict codes" that serve to orient the newcomers and make confinement more bearable.

▪ There is a greater amount of homosexuality among female prisoners than among male prisoners—much of it reflected in manners and dress. In most cases homosexuality is practiced by women who were not homosexual outside and who will go back to men once outside of prison. These women are the so-called jailhouse turnout. There is no evidence that any of these relationships are coercive in the way that young male prisoners are sometimes pressured into homosexuality. Estimates of the total amount vary—but most of the inmates themselves believed at least 50 percent were involved, and many estimates of staff and inmates ran from 60 to 75 percent.

▪ This temporary homosexuality can be understood as a response to and compensation for the pains of imprisonment itself. Without the emotional support and help they get from families and lovers in the outside world, without the organization and experience that male prisoners have, the female inmates turn to individual attachments.

Prison is one of the more extreme examples of the "total institution" that Erving Goffman describes graphically in his book *Asylums:*

> The recruit comes into the establishment with a conception of himself made possible by certain stable social arrangements in his home world. Upon entrance, he is

immediately stripped of the support provided by these arrangements . . . he begins a series of abasements, degradations, humiliations, and profanations of self. His self is systematically, if often unintentionally, mortified.

Soon the former identities and associations—sweetheart, daughter, mother, wife—seem to become unreal and appear to have happened long ago. New labels become relevant—prisoner, inmate, drug addict, murderer, thief—labels which are more damaging to women than they are to men.

Western culture is inclined to be more protective toward women, and generally will not justify treating them as harshly as it might the allegedly more aggressive, dangerous males. Proportionately, women are so much less often arrested, tried, convicted and sentenced that the effect is all the greater when a woman is imprisoned.

Upon arrival at the prison the women are questioned and told what personal belongings they can keep. Jewelry and rings with precious stones are taken away. Underwear becomes a matter of official regulation—inmates may keep their own only when: (1) pastel—not red, "a symbol of homosexuality", and (2) unpadded "to prevent narcotics from being smuggled in."

The prisoner is fingerprinted and photographed and takes a supervised bath. Then comes the most embarrassing admission experience, a pelvic examination in a room with other women—an examination not for medical reasons, but for the discovery of narcotics and other prohibited goods. Finally the new arrival is issued temporary clothing to get her to the reception cottage. Shortly after that she receives a medical examination and is issued regular clothing.

One great difference between this institution and male prisons is that the women can keep a great many personal articles and clothing, including: coats, jackets, raincoats (all "no quilting, padding or fur"), sweaters ("no turtle-neck,

V-neck, or tight slipover"), gowns or pajamas, bathrobes ("no quilting or padding"), shoes ("low heels, bedroom, thongs, tennis"), simple costume jewelry—earrings, necklaces, scatter pins, bracelets, non-electric clocks, dark glasses, unopened cigarettes, suitcases ("no larger than 18x26 inches"), unfinished knitting and light hand-sewing material, toothbrush, hair rollers, and so forth.

Thus the complete stripping of all personal possessions that takes place in male prisons does not occur here, and the pains of the admission experience are mitigated slightly.

New inmates report two major initial emotions: surprise and fear. Much of the surprise turns out to be pleasant— the physical conditions are not as bad as they had feared— a measure of the apprehension they bring to prison:

"It's less difficult than I assumed; it's not like home but it's going to be easy compared to how I thought it would be. It's neater, cleaner, you got combs, towels, etc. If you just have patience. The girls as a whole are not rough or tough; they've got more heart than the people on the outside. We can talk to each other. I'll tell you what scared me—that rolled wire. I said, 'Take one last look' (at the outside), but the inside looked better than the parks in the city."

Despite the favorable impression conveyed by the attractive grounds, fear and apprehension are characteristic of the newcomer: fear of mistreatment, dread of the future and of prison life, and fear generated by uncertainty, aggravated by the fact that many rules and staff explanations are unclear.

Women are especially ill-prepared to cope with uncertainty. Outside they may be able to depend on families, husbands, and lovers who might have personal regard and respect for them. In prison they immediately become dependent on the staff, whose interest is professional and casual, and whose personalities and whims soon assume overwhelming importance. The staff controls almost all the necessities and comforts of their daily lives—including many which are considered basic, inviolable and personal, outside—as well as being able to affect the length of time served. The inmates feel that the rules are what the staff interpret them to be, and that the prisoners are treated like children:

"You are constantly addressed as though you were either a mental case or a child—most of the staff here formerly worked in mental institutions or taught school. They feel it necessary to constantly nag you. The routine is the same from day to day. There is little to challenge a four-year-old, much less an adult. You lose the power, if you're not careful, to make even a small decision, or harbor an original thought."

Imprisonment is also more severe for women than for men because it is much more unusual. Female inmates generally have not come up through the "sandlots of crime" or had experience in training schools or reformatories, as have prisoners in penitentiaries for men. Of a sample of 293 female inmates, only 15 percent had ever been committed to juvenile training school, and 65 percent had never been in prison before. Although jail terms for drunkenness, prostitution, and petty theft are fairly frequent, for many women prison is a completely new experience.

Most women who come to prison are unsophisticated as criminals, and their lack of prior experience in doing time has not prepared them to suffer the rigors of confinement. They are more vulnerable than men to the indignities, degradation, and loss of privacy and identity that take place in prison. These pains strike the new prisoner, fresh from arrest, trial, and conviction, with particular force.

There is a further psychological pain of prison which is

particularly severe for a woman who is a mother—leaving her children. A man can serve time knowing that although the family may have great difficulty without his income, his wife can still care for the children. The imprisoned mother, however, loses her ability to fill what is, in our society, her most important function. This is psychologically meaningful even though many of the women had been sexually promiscuous and had more than one marriage. The mother is not only concerned with separation from the children but worries about how they will be cared for while her husband works. While she is in prison, unable to interfere, her children's care may be taken over by the municipality; or her husband may look for another woman to act as mother.

This concern was apparent when inmates were asked on a questionnaire, "To what aspect of prison life do you find it hardest to adjust?" Forty-three percent checked "absence of home and family"—four times as many as checked any other answer. The data also indicate that this frustration is not appreciably lessened as the length of time served increases.

During the early period, when the psychological pains of imprisonment are most acute, the inmate most needs emotional support. One described her feelings as follows:

"Knowing I was going to be sentenced here, I made every effort to see that my first week would be one of total escape . . . The morning of my sentence I took every form of pill I could manage to get, smoked as much marijuana as my mind could possibly stand and still manage to receive my sentence as a lady. The shock of hearing the inevitable penetrated with the same force as though I had indulged nothing but my common sense. However, the after-effects were successful . . . I managed to float through my first four days, depressed when I was awake, but slept most of the time. I felt as though I had been pushed off the edge of the world, and in many ways, it still seems this way."

Apprehensive and bewildered, new arrivals are most in need of information and reassurance about what to do and what to expect. Most of what they get comes from other inmates—in jail, enroute to the prison, and in the receiving unit. There are enough returned parole violators and second or third termers to give the new arrivals information that the staff and orientation program do not provide. Eventually they do learn the answers to most of their questions; eventually they may also find emotional support.

The most important question for each woman, however, is one that neither staff nor other inmates can answer: How long will she serve? The indeterminate sentencing laws of the state—generally considered a step forward in penology, make it not only impossible to know when one can be paroled, but, until actual appearance before the parole board, even when eligibility will be considered. Waiting to get a definite sentence becomes more trying than waiting for a release date.

If the indeterminate sentencing law results in uncertainty, the philosophy of "individual treatment" compounds it by adding inconsistency.

Individual treatment is based on the proposition that all individuals and the circumstances surrounding their actions differ. Therefore, treatment must take into account the peculiarities and needs of each person. The classification and disciplinary committees, and the parole board, may deal differently with women who have committed the same offense or violated the same prison rule.

Since these decisions are reached in private, few staff members and no inmates know the bases for most of them, and the suspicion arises that whim, prejudice, or favoritism decide many. In addition, the important decisions are made by upper-level personnel and committees who have little sustained contact with individual prisoners. The inmates feel that the staff members who know and understand them best, the cottage and work-crew supervisors, are those who are least able to do anything to help them.

Not knowing how long they must stay, not knowing what to expect from individual staff members, administrative committees or the parole board, inmates feel lost and out of sight of landmarks. Sociologists refer to this lack of standards, rules, and guidelines as *anomie*.

Male prisoners are subject to anomie, too; but they fight prison by working with others to set up a common defense against the personal degradation, self-mortification, and loss of identity. They have developed rules and maxims covering these adaptations, and these make up the so-called inmate code. New arrivals find information available from inmate "politicians" and "right guys," and scarce goods are available from "merchants." Criminal behavior is rationalized and justified; methods and techniques for getting scarce goods and services are made known; and ways to deal with staff and fellow inmates are detailed. The code provides a philosophy for doing time that makes it more bearable; and the inmate social organization provides the mechanisms for assuring conformity to the code.

The standards of the men stress hostility toward staff, and fundamental cynicism toward the world. By contrast the women are squares. Few are cynical in the same way as men prisoners, or as sophisticated in crime, its lingo, or its rationalizations.

Evidence of how naive they are was illustrated during a search for forbidden material in the housing units. The inmates were told they would have several minutes warning before their rooms were searched to allow them to flush illegal items down the toilets. Interpreting this order as a break, they did as told instead of searching out other ways to hide or get rid of goods. The sewage from each cottage was then filtered, permitting the staff to ascertain the nature, amount, and general location of contraband materials. There are undoubtedly some male prisoners who compare in gullibility, but not as many as in the women's prison.

In summary, it can be said that female prisoners suffer most of the psychological pains that men do, in addition to some distinctly their own. However, because they have distinctive needs and different histories of criminality, the kinds of adaptations they make vary somewhat from those found in prisons for men.

There are many personal reactions to stress, and each may come in a number of forms. Psychological withdrawal is one. Goffman describes another as "colonization"—becoming so well attuned to prison that it becomes "home." Revolt is a third. There are troublemakers at the women's prison, but most of them seem to be either emotionally disturbed or are homosexuals trying to promote or protect their interests. It is evident, however, that the principal adaptation utilized by these female prisoners is the homosexual liaison. This adaptation reflects the most severe deprivation of confinement for women—emotional deprivation. Most of the women interviewed saw this need as motivating most homosexual affairs:

"Why do girls 'turn out?' They need to be loved, everybody has to have someone."

"There's a lot of homosexuality because women are more emotional. They find in a jail that they have to depend on themselves. They need someone to talk to, so they get friendly, which leads to sexual intimacy."

One inmate described for a female interviewer how she

(the inmate) might have approached the interviewer if the interviewer had been a newly arrived inmate:

"Let's say you've four children; you're not a criminal, but passed some bad checks and you come in with everyone that matters so far away . . . Once I know you don't play, then I begin to build a friendship, knowing all the while what's going on, although you do not. Maybe we like the same music, poetry, or other things of common interest. We spend lots of time together, and then I leave you alone for a week maybe playing with someone else. You'll miss me. You'll want to know if I'm mad at you. You'll miss me—after all, we've filled up a lot of time together. By this time you like me, and you're wondering. 'What's it like? What would my people think? What would I have to do? Is it really so sick?' By then I'm half being your friend again. The pressure's on. Then one day the time is right; the scene is right; I'm full of emotion (as all women are), and you say to yourself. 'She really loves me. I care for her. surely it's not a wrong thing . . .' "

A related question here is whether heterosexual deprivation is a major factor leading to homosexuality. Some staff members believe so, but inmate opinion does not support them. The question asking which aspect of imprisonment was the most difficult to bear included among the alternative answers: "Lack of sexual contact with men." Of the 293 women questioned a total of only five selected this answer, as compared to over 120 for "Absence of home and family." Not one of those questioned in interviews thought that sex hunger was of primary importance in influencing her own homosexual affairs—or of those of anyone she knew. In addition, most homosexuality first occurs at the beginning of the sentence. Presumably, it is not at the time that the frustrations arising from the absence of heterosexual contacts is most acute. It is, however, at the beginning of her sentence that the inmate is most in need of comfort, support, and reassurance.

Homosexuality involves more than a change in the gender of the love object. For some women it represents a dramatic inversion of sexual role. These shifts are manifest in the principal homosexual roles played by women. The most obvious of them is the *butch, stud broad* or *drag butch*. She is the counterpart of the male and, ideally, acts in an aggressive manner and is the active sexual partner. Her hair is close-cropped or worn in "pixie" or "D.A." styles; she wears no makeup; her legs are unshaven; she usually wears pedal pushers, or if a dress, the belt is worn low on the hips. Masculine gait, manner of smoking, and other gestures are adopted. A variation of this is the woman who dresses femininely, but acts aggressively and plays the dominant role in her homosexual relationship. Many of the jailhouse turnouts who are butches are singularly unattractive, according to some of the criteria used to judge feminine attractiveness in our society. Many are overweight or underweight, have skin disorders, or appear unusually wiry or muscular. In addition, interview and personal record data suggest that the experience of many butches with males has often been unhappy. These severely unattractive women, and the women possessing aggressive personality traits and inclined toward masculine habits and demeanor, express themselves in the butch role when these predisposing factors are combined with the experience of imprisonment. The role of the butch in the prison community thus seems to be an effort to solve a variety of problems and conflicts of which adjustment to imprisonment is one.

The complementary role to the butch is the *femme*. It is less difficult to describe and to understand the role of the femme because she often does in the homosexual affair what she did in heterosexual relationships. She continues to play the role often expected of women: to be relatively more submissive and passive in sexual relations, to be dependent, and to provide housekeeping services. The role of the femme provides relief from the need to fend for oneself in a strange and threatening environment. This role provides for the establishment of supportive relationships similar to those which characterized relationships with fathers, husbands, or lovers.

The newly arrived female prisoner is placed in a situation in which any source of relieving the pains of imprisonment holds great attraction. The old supports from the outside world are gone; the groupings and organization that help men do time do not exist for women. Despite efforts of the staff to cope with the problem, there remain for many women only the comfort and help that can come from a close association with another individual. And the persons who are quickest, most available, and most aggressive in offering information and solace are homosexual. Homosexual liaisons appear initially to satisfy needs which are otherwise not met, and the form which is taken suggests that the most severe strain of imprisonment for women is emotional deprivation.

The term "jailhouse turnout" is a way of summing up this adjustment to a stressful situation. The indications are that most prison homosexuality is temporary and transitional with heterosexual relationships being resumed upon release. The problem for women's prisons is finding a socially acceptable substitute for the emotional support that women inmates derive from their lesbian liaisons.

January 1964

Pornography- Raging Menace or Paper Tiger?

WILLIAM SIMON/JOHN H. GAGNON

Since the task of defining pornography has fallen more and more on the Supreme Court—and since not much research exists on what effect pornography has on the social actions of individuals—what standard is the court using?

The Supreme Court seems to be erecting a more complex standard for judging pornography to replace the old concern with individual morality. Some interesting insights into the confusion surrounding the topic can be drawn from three court decisions of March 21, 1966: *Ginzburg* v. *United States, Mishkin* v. *New York,* and *Memoirs of a Woman of Pleasure* v. *Massachusetts.* Although this set of decisions was almost immediately accorded distinction as a landmark by the public, the Nine Old Men themselves did not seem quite so sure of the meaning of the affair. The justices produced among them 14 separate opinions in the three cases. Only three judges were in the majority in

137

all cases. The decisions were divided, respectively, 5-4, 6-3, and 6-3.

Ginzburg is the key decision. The court reversed the suppression of *Memoirs,* better known as *Fanny Hill,* under the Roth test of 1957—that is, "whether to the average person, applying contemporary standards, the dominant theme of the material taken as a whole appeals to a prurient interest." The conviction of Edward Mishkin, owner of the Main Stem and Midget book stores in New York City, was upheld. In the words of the court, Mishkin "was not prosecuted for anything he said or believed, but for what he did." What he did was commission, publish, and sell such illustrated books as *Mistress of Leather, Cult of Spankers,* and *Fearful Ordeal in Restraintland* for an audience interested in sadomasochism, transvestitism, fetishism.

Ralph Ginzburg was being tried on postal charges of obscenity for three publications: *The Housewife's Handbook of Selective Promiscuity,* an issue of the biweekly newsletter *Liaison,* and a volume of the hardbound magazine *Eros.* In this case the court departed from earlier rulings by considering not the obscenity of the specific items, but rather the appeal to prurient interest made in the advertising campaigns. The court remarked, "Where the purveyor's sole emphasis is on the sexually provocative aspects of his publications, that fact may be decisive in the determination of 'obscenity.' "

To the court, one of the proofs of Ginzburg's motives was his request for second-class mailing privileges at Intercourse or Blue Ball, Pennsylvania, before obtaining them at Middlesex, New Jersey. One of the indicators of the social worth of *Fanny Hill,* conversely, was the translation of the book into braille by the Library of Congress.

Three of the justices voting for reversal filed written dissents in which they argued that the court was creating a new crime—that of pandering, exploitation, or titillation—which Ginzburg could not have known existed when he committed it. Furthermore, the dissenters said, if a statute creating such a crime had come before the court, it would be found unconstitutional.

It is the Ginzburg decision that gives us the primary thread to follow in seeking to understand "obscenity" as it is now seen by the Supreme Court and the sexual arousal caused by what is conventionally termed pornography. With this decision the court has moved—in a way that may be inimical to the conception of law as abstract principle—toward a more realistic determination of the factors relevant to triggering a sexual response. The court's sociological discovery—whether intentional or not—is that in sex the context of the representation is significant. That is, sex as a physical object or symbolic representation has no power outside a context in which the erotic elements are reinforced or made legitimate.

In doing this, the court did not change the rules under which any work will be considered outside its context. If a book is charged—as *Fanny Hill* was—with being obscene under the Roth decision, it will be treated in exactly the same way as it would have been in the past. When aspects of the context of advertising or sale—the acts of labeling—are included in the original charges, then the Ginzburg rules will be applied. This was demonstrated in the court's decision this May on a number of girlie magazines. Obscenity convictions against the magazines were overturned because, as the court stated, "In none was there evidence of the sort of pandering which the court found significant in *Ginzburg v. United States.*"

Whether the majority of the court was aware of the significance of the change it made in the definition of obscenity is not clear. From the tone of the opinions, it is obvious the court felt it was dealing with a problem of nuisance behavior—not only to the public, but to the court itself— quite analogous to keeping a goat in a residential area, or urinating in public. By making the promotion of the work a factor in determining its obscenity, the court was reinforcing the right of the person to keep his mailbox clean and private, not to mention the likelihood that it was cutting down the amount of misleading advertising.

The court apparently considers pornography to have two major dimensions. The first can be defined as dealing with sexual representations that are offensive to public morality or taste, which concerned the court most importantly in the Ginzburg case. The second centers on the effect of pornography on specific individuals or classes, which is the focus of most public discussions and prior court decisions on pornography. This dimension was mentioned only twice in the array of decisions of 1966, but much of the confusion in discussions of pornography reflects a difficulty in distinguishing between these dimensions or a tendency to slip from one to the other without noting the change.

The first dimension—offenses to a public morality—not only appears more objective, but also has a cooler emotional tone. The problem becomes one of tolerating a public nuisance, or defining what constitutes a public nuisance. This issue becomes complex because the heterogeneity of an urban society makes it difficult to arrive at a consensus on what the limits of public morality might be. We might also add the complicating factor of our society's somewhat uneven libertarian tradition that affirms the theoretical existence of the right to subscribe to minority versions of morality. These obviously touch upon important issues of constitutional freedoms. As important as the implicit issues may be, however, the explicit issue is public nuisance, a misdemeanor, usually bringing only a fine or, at most, up to a year in the county jail. Talk of offense to public morality or public taste is relatively remote from the old fears of serious damage to the community or its members.

The second dimension—effects upon persons exposed to pornographic productions—generates more intense emotions. Claims are made that exposure to pornography results in infantile and regressive approaches to sexuality that can feed an individual's neuroses or, at the other extreme, that exposure tends to fundamentally and irreversibly corrupt and deprave. The latter argument asserts that exposure to pornography either awakens or creates sexual appetites that can only be satisfied through conduct that is dangerous to society. More simply stated: Pornography is a trigger mechanism that has a high probability of initiating dangerous, antisocial behavior. There also exists what can be called a major counterargument to these, but one that shares with them a belief in the effectiveness of pornography. This argument is that pornography serves as an alternative sexual outlet, one that releases sexual tensions that might otherwise find expression in dangerous, antisocial behavior. For the proponents of this view, pornography is seen as a safety valve or a psychological lightning rod.

The very act of labeling some item as pornographic or obscene creates a social response very close to that brought on by pornography itself. The act of labeling often generates sexual anticipation centered on fantasies about the business of pornography and the erotic character of those who produce it. How else could such benign and hardly erotic productions as family-planning pamphlets and pictures of human birth have come under the shadow of the pornography laws? As with other unconventional sexual expressions, in public consideration of pornography even the dreary details of production, distribution, and sale are matters for erotic speculation. This simplification—defining as totally sexual that which is only marginally connected with sexuality—is perhaps one of the major sources of the public concern over pornography.

Labeling can also be done by individuals, who can thus make pornographic the widest range of materials—*Studs Lonigan, Fanny Hill, Playboy,* the Sears Roebuck catalog. This ability leads to the assumption that sexual fantasy and its agent, pornography, have a magical capacity to commit men to overt sexual action. In this view the sexual impulse lies like the beast in every man, restrained only by the slight fetters of social repression. This assumption, founded on the Enlightenment's notion of a social contract, underpins most of our discussions of sex and its sideshow, pornography.

These serious views of pornography can lead directly to the formulation of an empirically testable question. Unfortunately, no one has provided an answer acceptable as the outcome of reliable and systematic research procedures.

Of the data that are available on the effects of pornography, the best remain those provided by the investigations of the Institute for Sex Research. Kinsey and his associates indicate that the majority of males in our society are exposed, at one time or another, to "portrayals of sexual action." So are a smaller proportion of females. Further, 77 percent of males who had exposure to "portrayals of sexual action" reported being erotically aroused, while only 32 percent of women reported feelings of arousal. What is significant is that, arousal notwithstanding, no dramatic changes of behavior appeared to follow for those reporting both exposure and arousal. Perhaps even more significant is the fact that Paul H. Gebhard and his colleagues in their book *Sex Offenders* report:

> It would appear that the possession of pornography does not differentiate sex offenders from nonsex offenders. Even the combination of ownership plus strong sexual

arousal from the material does not segregate the sex offender from other men of a comparable social level. Summing up their feeling that pornography is far from being a strong determinant of sexual behavior and that the use of pornography tends to be a derivative of already existing sexual commitments, the authors observe: "Men make the collections, collections do not make the men."

However, given the intensity and frequency with which the argument of pornography's corrupting powers is raised, one might wonder whether thinking about pornography has not itself given rise to sexual fantasies, developing an image of men and women as being more essentially sexual than they may in fact be.

The two major dimensions—public offense versus public corruption—result in two different images of the pornographer. Projected through the rhetoric of public corruption we see him as someone self-consciously evil, a representative of the antichrist, the Communist conspiracy, or at the very least, the Mafia. We also tend to see him in terms of the obscenity of ill-gotten wealth as he deals in commodities that are assumed to generate high prices.

Thought of as a public nuisance, he appears in somewhat more realistic hues. Here we find not a sinister villain but a grubby businessman producing a minor commodity for which there is a limited market and a marginal profit and which requires that he live in a marginal world. Here our collective displeasure may be derived from his association with a still greater obscenity—economic failure. However, whether the pornographer is Mephistopheles or a Willie Loman, he is one of the few in our society whose public role is overtly sexual, and that is perhaps reason enough to abandon any expectations of rationality in public discussions of the role.

We tend to ignore the social context within which pornography is used and from which a large part of its significance for the individual consumer derives. The stag film is an excellent case in point. Out of context it is rarely more than a simple catalogue of the limited sexual resources of the human body. Stag films are rarely seen by females and most commonly by two kinds of male groups: those living in group housing in colleges or universities and those belonging to upper-lower class and lower-middle class voluntary social groups. The stag film serves both similar and different functions for the two major categories of persons who see them.

For the college male they are a collective representation of mutual heterosexual concerns and—to a lesser degree—they instruct in sexual technique. For this group the exposure is either concurrent with, or prior to, extensive sociosexual experience. Exposure comes later in life for the second group: after marriage or, at the very least, after the development of sociosexual patterns. For this audience the group experience itself provides validation of sexual appetites in social milieus where other forms of validation, such as extramarital activity, are severely sanctioned. The films primarily reinforce masculinity and only indirectly reinforce heterosexuality. This reinforcement of heterosexuality is reflected in the way the films portray the obsessive myths of masculine sexual fantasy. They emphasize, for example, that sexual encounters can happen at any moment, to anyone, around almost any corner—a belief that is a close parallel to the romantic love fantasy so very characteristic of female arousal. In the case of the male, however, sex replaces love as the central element. These films also reaffirm the myth of a breed of women who are lusty and free in both surrender and enjoyment. Last, given the kind of social context within which the films are shown, there is little reason to assume that their sexual arousal is not expressed through appropriate sexual or social actions.

Pictorial representations of sexual activity lend themselves to the same approach. Unlike films and more like written materials, their use is essentially private. Nonetheless, patterns of use remain congruent with other patterns of social life and process; they represent anything but the triggering mechanisms through which the social contract is nullified and raging, unsocial lust (whatever that might be) is unleashed. The major users of pictorial erotica are adolescent males. If these materials have any use, it is as an aid to masturbation. There is no evidence, however, that the availability of dirty pictures increases masturbatory rates among adolescents. This is a period in life when masturbatory rates are already extremely high, particularly for middle class adolescents. Indeed, in the absence of hard-core pornography, the boys create their own stimulation from mail-order catalogues, magazine ads, and so on. In middle class circles, many young men and the majority of females may grow up without ever having seen hard-core pornography.

If exposure to this kind of pornography, while facilitating masturbation, does not substantially affect masturbatory rates, it is still possible that such materials may shape the content of the masturbatory fantasy in ways that create or reinforce commitments to sexual practices that are harmful to the individual or to others. In this area little is known. It may be observed that most pornographic materials share with the masturbatory fantasy a sense of omnipotence, but the acts represented are rarely homosexual, nor are they sadistic beyond the general levels of violence common in contemporary kitsch. Once again, one suspects a reinforcing or facilitating function rather than one of initiation or creation.

The pornographic book, in contrast to photographs and films, represents a very different social situation. Few books are read aloud in our society, and it is very unlikely that this would occur with a book of descriptions of overt sexual activity. In fact, prosecutors take advantage of this by reading allegedly obscene books aloud in court with the aim of embarrassing the jury into a guilty verdict. The privately consumed erotic book merely provides fantasy content or reinforcement of fantasy that is already established. Few books lead to overt action of any kind, and the erotic book is unlikely to be an exception.

The most difficult problem in considering pornography is the fringeland found on newsstands: the pulp books, national tabloids, men's magazines, and pinup collections which line the racks in drugstores, bus stations, and rail and air terminals. The girlie magazines are often under attack for nude pictures. The current magic line of censorship is pubic hair, though recently it was the bare breast or exposed nipple. Not so very long ago, navels were ruthlessly airbrushed away and Jane Russell's cleavage was an issue in gaining the censor's approval of the movie "Outlaw." The Gay Nineties were made gayer with pinups of strapping beauties clad in tights revealing only the bare flesh of face and hands.

In our era the pulp book freely describes most sexual activity with some degree of accuracy, although less explicitly and more metaphorically than hard-core pornographic pulp books. Such books are clearly published for their capacity to elicit sexual arousal, and they are purchased by an audience that knows what it is buying.

To view these examples of fringe pornography exclusively in terms of a sexual function might well be misleading. Since we tend to overestimate the significance of sexual activity, we see the trends of representation in these works as indicators of sexual behavior in the community. An increase in works about homosexual love is taken as an indication of an incipient homosexual revolution or even as the cause of a homosexual revolution. If we find more books about adultery, sadomasochism, or fast-living teenagers, we believe that there must be more adulterers, sadomasochists, and fast-living teenagers in our midst. With a dubious logic reminiscent of primitive magic, many believe that if the number of such representations increases, so will the frequency of such acts, and conversely that the way to cut down on this antisocial behavior is to suppress the pornographic representations.

In the fringeland there is a greater attempt to place sexual activity in the context of a social script, with a greater concern for nonsexual social relations and social roles, and a more direct treatment of appropriate social norms. Some part of this, particularly its common trait of compulsive moralizing, is an attempt to establish a spurious —but defensible under the Roth decision—"redeeming context." This may also represent the producer's awareness that more than simple lust is involved, that the reader may bring to the work a complex of motives, many of which are nonsexual.

For example, the psychiatrist Lionel Ovesey links some of the fantasies of his homosexual patients not to their sexual commitments, but to their problems of managing other personal relations, particularly in their jobs. The management of dominance or aggression in nonsexual spheres of life or the management of ideologies and moralities of social mobility may be the organizing mechanisms of such fantasies while sexuality provides an accessible and powerful imagery through which these other social tensions may be vicariously acted upon. Possibly it is overly simplistic to view this marginal pornography merely as something exclusively sexual.

These items at the fringeland are of most concern in the formulation of community standards. The girlie magazine and the pulp book are visible and priced within the range of the mass market. The hardcover book available at a high price in a bookstore may well cause no comment until it goes on the drugstore racks in paperback. Because such items are sold at breaks in transportation or in locations that tap neighborhood markets, they are the most visible portion of the problem and are the source of the discontent among those who are committed to censorship.

The dilemma, then, becomes the formulation of community standards, and this has been the dilemma of the courts themselves. One interesting attempt to strengthen enforcement of conservative standards is the interpretation of federal law to allow prosecution of a seller in the jurisdiction in which materials are received rather than in the ones from which they are mailed. Thus in the rather liberal jurisdiction of New York, where the sale of obscene materials must be compared in the mind of the judge with all the other kinds of crimes that come before him, the seller may well be seen as a small-timer, his crime a misdemeanor. However, in a rural jurisdiction where religious standards are more conservative and a pornography offense is viewed more seriously—especially when compared with the strayed cows and traffic violations that make up the most of the court docket—the seller is a heinous criminal.

The Supreme Court may wish to establish a national standard, allowing some jurisdictions to be more liberal but none to be more conservative. Thus the Supreme Court may build a floor under the right of materials to be protected under the First Amendment, at the same time constraining, through the use of the Ginzburg decision, the importation of materials through wide mailing campaigns into conservative communities. In its more recent decision, the court indicated—somewhat Delphically—that its concern in the future would be with three areas, none of them directly concerned with the content of any works charged as pornographic. These were sales of smut to minors, obtrusive presentation, and "pandering" *a la* Ginzburg. The court's decisions, however, may well be too conservative in a period when a national society is being created through penetration by the mass media of larger and larger elements of the society. Indeed, it is likely that most legal revolutions have been imposed from above and that communities will fall back to the set floor, if allowed to do so.

Pornography is as elusive as mercury. That of the past often no longer fills the bill. The use and users of contemporary pornography vary. Indeed, it might be said that sex itself would not change if there were no more pornography. Pornography is only a minor symptom of sexuality and of very little prominence in people's minds most of the time. Even among those who might think about it most, it results either in masturbation or in the "collector" instinct.

What is most important about pornography is not that it is particularly relevant to sexuality, but that it elicits very special treatment when it confronts the law. In this confrontation the agencies of criminal justice, and especially the courts, behave in a very curious manner that is quite dangerous for the freedom of ideas as they might be expressed in other zones of activity such as politics, religion, or the family. Our best protection in this regard has been the very contradictory character of the courts which carefully excludes the consideration of sexual ideas from the general test of the expression of ideas: Do they give rise to a clear and present danger? Our problem is not that pornography represents such a danger—it is far too minor a phenomenon for that—but that the kind of thinking prevalent in dealing with pornography will come to be prevalent in controlling the advocacy of other ideas as well.

July/August 1967

FURTHER READING SUGGESTED BY THE AUTHORS:

The Other Victorians by Steven Marcus (New York City: Basic Books, Inc., 1964). The social, literary, and psychoanalytic study of Victorian pornography by a distinguished critic.

Hustlers, Beats, and Others by Ned Polsky (Chicago: Aldine Publishing Co., 1967). The most explicit treatment of pornography from a sociological perspective.

Language and Silence: Essays in Language, Literature and the Inhuman edited by G. Steiner (New York City: Atheneum Publishers, 1967). See "Night Words" by George Steiner, a consideration of the impact of pornography on public language and private fantasy.

Eros Denied, Part III by Wayland Young (New York City: Grove Press, Inc., 1964). A defense of the role of pornography in society.

COM
COM